Fortunate's
Unfortunate Fortunes

Fortunate's Unfortunate Fortunes

The True Story of a Ugandan Woman's Heroic Journey in America

FORTUNATE HIGGINS, BA, MPS

ISBN: 1546514317
ISBN 13: 9781546514312
Library of Congress Control Number: 2017907638
CreateSpace Independent Publishing Platform
North Charleston, South Carolina

Contents

Introduction

I am not perfect; neither am I a saint. Although my story is totally different, sometimes I wonder whether my whole life was shaped by that of my childhood hero, Josephine Bakhita. My father named me Fortunate. As a little girl, my parents gave me a beautiful illustrated children's autobiography book about Josephine Bakhita that I treasured very much. Her name, Bakhita, also means "fortunate."

While growing up I wanted to be like her even though her life involved a series of unfortunate events. She was from a small village in Sudan. When she was about eight years old, while she was playing with her friend in the bushes near her village, some Arab slave traders kidnapped her and sold her into slavery. In shock, she could not remember her name or the village she came from. Her owner named her Bakhita. She was sold three times to different slave owners, who often whipped her. She was sold the second time to a Turkish general after she got in trouble for accidentally breaking her master's expensive vase. Bakhita and other new slaves were forced to be tattooed, a painful procedure that, according to S. Wallace, "involved tracing detailed patterns on the body and arms of each slave, then going over the patterns with sharp razor. When the cutting was done, salt was rubbed into bleeding wounds every day, so scars would form as they slowly healed." Bakhita's body was covered with scars that she would bear for the rest of her life.

Her luck came when she was sold a third time at the age of fourteen, this time to an Italian consul. Her new master treated her very well, and she lived happily. Two years later her master took her along to Italy. She would experience yet further challenges due to the color of her skin. On arrival in Italy, her master gave her to his friend, whose wife had passed away during childbirth. She became the nanny of his little girl, Mimmina, who grew attached to her.

After spending some time in a convent at a boarding school where she had temporarily been placed with the little girl while her master was away, she was introduced to Christianity. She decided to get baptized and pursue a religious path. She got in trouble; her master took her to court for refusing to return to him to continue her duties as a nanny. Since slavery was illegal in Italy, the courts gave her freedom. She became a nun and spent the rest of her life in Italy, where she died and was buried. Pope John Paul II canonized her as a saint in 2000. Details about Josephine Bakhita's true story can be found in the children's book *Saint Bakhita of Sudan* and the movie *From Slavery to Saint*.

On the other hand, I also wonder whether my last name influenced my misfortunes. My great uncle Col. Ozoo Joseph named me Drateru. The name Drateru means "waiting for death." I was born while my great uncle was a political prisoner on death row in Luzira Maximum Prison in Uganda. He had served the country during Uganda's infamous dictator president Idi Amin's regime. After Amin's government was overthrown, those who served in his cabinet and didn't go into exile were imprisoned. My great uncle was one of them, but he was released years later. He died several years later of natural causes.

Some people say that names can influence one's life. I grew to hate my last name as I began experiencing unfortunate situations in my life. Although the meaning of my name Drateru was not meant for me, I couldn't help but wonder what a combination it was to be Fortunate and await death.

Part One

WHO THE BLEEP DID I MARRY?

One

My Childhood

I was born and raised in Uganda. I had a good childhood until about the age of twelve. My father Mr. Peter Vunia had studied and worked as a nurse in Great Britain in the 1970s. Upon his return he established a good life for himself and his family. He was Uganda's passport control officer signing the Ugandan passports. He also owned one of the leading mixed farms in Uganda. A mixed farm is an agricultural system in which a farmer conducts a combination of different agricultural practices such as cash-crop production, poultry, and dairy farming. Our farm, Penia Mixed Farm, mostly produced cotton, watermelon, livestock which included piggery, dairy, and poultry (raising layer chickens for the purpose of eggs) farming. My mother, Mrs. Rose Vunia, was a prison officer at Luzira Maximum Prison in the 1970s and early 1980s when I was born. She later transferred to serve as an administrator of the women's prison in Arua, Uganda. Together my mom and dad had five children (four sons and one daughter—me). I also have stepsiblings, whom I love dearly. At my father's request, my mother quit her job and moved to the village to become a full-time, stay-at-home mom between 1989 and 1990. Life was good, and I was pretty much a daddy's princess showered with gifts and so much love.

My father was the type of dad who enjoyed singing to his children. He nicknamed his kids and composed special songs for them. He called me Oli, a short form of my middle name Oliver. He named me Oliver and my elder brother Victor after Olive and Vic Marston, the British couple who hosted him during his years in England back in the 1970's. He would sing a special song to me with my name every time he arrived at the gate of our home. That was how I would know he was home. I would sing back to him, and run to welcome him. He was very gentle with me, and never punished me, not even once. He made me feel very special being the only girl amongst four boys by my mother.

I saw my father punish one of my brothers once because of me. Luke, my eldest brother had special needs as a result of cerebral malaria that he suffered from as a child. One day in the late 1980's the people in our village boarded our truck to go to my aunt's husband's funeral. I was watching from a distance as they boarded the vehicle. My brother had wanted to go too, but he had been told no, so he was unhappy. When he saw me standing there he ordered me to go home, but I insisted I wanted to see mommy get on the truck. He got angry and started chasing me, and beating me as he dragged me on the ground for about one hundred meters towards our home. As he was beating me there was a plane in the air about to land. Our village is located near Arua airfield, and my dad often travelled by air to and from Kampala city to the town of Arua. I had no idea he would be arriving that day. In order to get my brother to stop, I cried and pointed at the plane that was landing, and told him dad was in it. I was going to report him to daddy when he arrived. That made my brother even more angry, and he beat me more. All the adults in the home were gone, so nobody was to stop him. He finally stopped on his own, and then left to go hang-out at our neighbor's. Shortly after he was gone, my dad arrived. He had indeed traveled in the plane that landed. When he arrived he sang my song as usual, but this time I didn't sing back to him. I just ran to welcome him. When he asked what was wrong I showed him my back that was bruised from being dragged on the ground. He was so angry that he went looking for my brother within the village. He found him at my great uncle's home and started beating him, but the women there stopped him. My father left and came home drunk that night. He told my mother what happened and went straight to my brother's room and beat him badly. From that day on my brother hated my dad and me. He barely ever spoke to me again throughout the rest of our lives spent together. I was also afraid to talk to him. At some point in my adulthood I attempted to mend our relationship but it was too late.

Our mother was Luke's favorite. He spoke my mother's language fluently. Most of her other children, including myself, did not. Her native language is different from that of my father's. She was Alur (Luo) by tribe, and my father was a Lugbara. Luke considered my mother's side of the family his true relatives. He enjoyed spending time with them.

My relationship with my father remains dear to me. Although he is not in the best of health at the present moment he still sings to me once in a while when I call home.

My relationship with my mother was quite the converse to that of my father's. She was never a nurturing parent to me. I'm not sure if it was because of her career background as a prison officer, but I disliked that rough part of her. She owned a special unbreakable stick made of a bamboo tree. It had a metallic tip and a round metallic bottom engraved with the logo of Ugandan emblem on it. She sometimes used this stick to beat my elder brother and me. She beat us even for the slightest mistakes. I was a very forgetful child that resulted in me receiving a lot more beatings, so I was often fearful of her. The beatings always occurred in my father's absence, so he was never aware of them. I think he would have been very unhappy with her if he ever found out. However, despite her critical parenting nature, she was very hardworking, intelligent, smart, independent, and she was the woman behind some of my father's successes. My parents both helped raise kids not their own.

As an adult I've grown closer to my mother and value our relationship more than ever. Despite her harshness to me as a child I did learn a lot from her. I love my mother dearly, and care for her deeply, but growing up I was not so fond of her as compared to my father.

I attended Christ the King Kindergarten in Arua for my nursery school. During that time the school was headed by white Italian missionary nuns, Sr. Teresa and Sr. Francesca. Everything about my nursery school was civilized. The school was nicely fenced in with a beautiful playground, well-organized classrooms stocked with different kinds of toys, and children's books. They served us healthy breakfast every morning, and we learned and danced to all kinds of nursery rhymes. After completing three years of nursery school, I joined Arua Hill Primary School to begin my primary education.

I was about five years old in 1986 when the current government of Uganda overthrew the then government of the country. The rumor of the war spread quickly, and most of the people in my hometown fled to the neighboring Democratic Republic of Congo. My father decided to take his whole family to hide in his farm several miles away past hills and heavily wooded lands. The farm was heavily surrounded by woods, which he probably thought would provide a safe place. Like the scene in *The Sound of Music* when Captain von Trapp fled with his family from Austria, I remember being tied on a bicycle carrier with extra luggage in a metallic basin with my stepbrother of about the same age and pushed for miles by my father and another relative whom I do not remember now. I remember them carrying us over their shoulders to cross a river that ran chest high. We made it safely to our farm.

For unknown reasons to me, my father did not stay, but I believe he ensured the family was safe and had everything we needed for that period. Although we were safe and had survived the war, we would experience one of the most traumatic robberies by thieves whom my family would later learn were former prisoners. These prisoners had at one time been brought to do some work on our farm and seized the opportunity to rob my family.

I was so young, but I can still remember that night. My family had just gone to bed. I shared my mom's bedroom with her and her toddler child. We slept on a mattress that was laid on the floor. My stepmother also shared her room with her two young children. We had just gone to bed when our two dogs started barking continuously. We then heard footsteps, a loud knock, and voices of strangers speaking in Swahili.

These robbers had guns and knives. They shot the dogs dead and kicked our main door open. The main house we lived in was built of mud and reeds but had a roof made of iron. The doors were not strong enough even when locked. My father had his own room that was kept locked because he was not around, and my older brothers and cousins shared a room of their own. After killing the dogs, the robbers got loud and demanded the door be opened.

With my mother's career background as a prison officer, she asked in Swahili, "*We nani?*" which means, "Who are you?"

Right away the robbers kicked the main door open and broke in. Some of them went to my stepmother's room, while others to my mother's. They demanded money, scattered everything in the house, and took valuable items. I was lying on the mattress when the robbers came into the room I shared with my mother. They rolled me off the mattress onto my mother, searching for money under the bed and everywhere in the room. They placed a knife on my mother's neck, demanding she give them money or they would kill her. My mother stayed firm and told them she did not have any money. Thankfully they did not badly harm her or any member of my family, but they proceeded to break the door to my dad's room in which he kept his locked briefcases. These briefcases required a PIN combination to open them, but the robbers used their knives to cut them open. They switched their footwear with that of my dad's, taking off their worn-out shoes and putting on my father's shoes. They then left with lots of valuable items that they stole from us.

My mother recognized one of the robbers as one of her former prisoners, but there was nothing she could do. The robbers stole so much stuff that they ended up dropping some on the way out. My family believed that if my father had been around during this robbery, he could've gotten killed. After this incident my family decided to move back home in the village. The war that had sent many into exile had come to an end, and life finally normalized.

In 1993 my father decided to take my younger stepsister and me to live with him in the city where he worked as Uganda's passport control officer. My mom and the rest of my siblings stayed in the village. While in the city, we lived in a three-bedroom, two-bathroom modern apartment with electricity and running water; we watched TV like kids of today. We had a maid to help with housework, and my father's driver was a police officer who served as his bodyguard. This was where I would attend part of my primary-school education until 1995, after my father was unfortunately involved in an accident that left him brain damaged.

After undergoing brain surgery, he lost his memory and had to learn our names and everything else afresh like a newborn baby. With the blink of an eye, we lost everything. The farm, the truck, the tractor, and all his other properties were mismanaged and repossessed by the bank. The two horses that worked on our farm died, and most of the animals disappeared. The chicken on our poultry farm aged out, got sick, and died. We had no choice but to move back to the village where my father resides to this day. The only house we had in the village was collapsing since my father had not fulfilled his plans to construct a new one.

Life suddenly became extremely difficult for us. I lacked school fees to continue with my education; my older brother at some point suggested I drop out of school after just completing an ordinary-level certificate of education to pursue primary-teaching education. But somehow something within me told me I was destined for higher education, so I didn't settle for that. I lacked decent clothing. At home we slept on reed mats laid on the floor; we shared blankets. My mother had to take a job with a nongovernmental organization as a facilitator to make ends meet. We were living in extreme poverty and struggling for the most part.

On moving back to the village, I joined Arua Hill Primary School for the remaining two years of my primary education. My school was about fifteen kilometers away from home. I commuted to school using a bicycle that I rode from my village through Arua Town's busy streets to get to my school. We were expected to be in class by 7:30 a.m., so I would leave home by dawn. If we were late by just a minute, we got whipped by the school principal who was also our math teacher. Whipping the students seemed to be one of his favorite things to do. He would write a math equation on the blackboard and randomly select a student to solve it. He often held a fresh stick from a branch of a tree and stood behind the student solving the math problem. If the student made a mistake or got the answer wrong, he would whip him or her on the back. The students were extremely afraid of him.

I had my one unforgettable experience with this principal when I showed up to school wearing rubber sandals, other than black closed shoes with white socks—which was part of our school uniform. I had just arrived and parked my bicycle under a tree. My principal had been watching me from a distance. He was holding a long stick in his hand as he waited for latecomers. As I walked toward my classroom, he pointed at me with the stick in his hand and yelled, "You! Come here!" In fear, I walked and stood in front of him. He commanded me to take off my sandals. He then went into his office and came out with razor blades that he handed to me. He ordered me to cut my sandals into pieces as he watched. The pair of sandals was made of hard rubber material. My hands bled as I cut them because I accidentally cut myself. I was left bare feet, and he didn't allow me to attend classes that day. I wandered around the school's football field as I waited for time to lapse so I could go home when other students did.

Fortunate's Unfortunate Fortunes

The year 1996 was my final year of attending primary school. My mom speculated that the long-distance commute from my village to my school might negatively impact my academic performance. So for that year, I was sent to live with my aunt who lived within Arua town, which was a shorter distance to my school. After hard work, I sat for the primary leaving examination administered by UNEB (Uganda National Examination Board) and passed with flying colors.

After successfully completing primary education, I attended Muni Girls Boarding Secondary School from 1997 through 2000. I was a popular student for my talent in fine arts. My artworks were used for demonstrations in upper classes. But I was often sent home because of my unpaid school fees. One day the school sent me home as usual due to the unpaid school fees. Upon my return my classmates informed me that my art teacher had been looking for me. He had wanted me to participate in a national art competition to design a millennium postage stamp for Uganda; the deadline was approaching. I completed the artwork in one day, handed it to my teacher, and forgot all about it. In December 1999 I met one of my classmates, who informed me that my artwork was on a postage stamp in the post office with my name on it. They were being sold for three hundred Ugandan shillings each. We went to the post office together, purchased a copy, and informed the regional postal manager that it was my work. After a follow-up, I was awarded three hundred thousand Ugandan shillings, which I used to pay part of my school fees for the following year. In the years to come, I participated in two other national/international art competitions—one with Uganda Human Rights, in which I won five hundred thousand UGX, and another with UNFPA (United Nations Population Fund), in which I won another five hundred thousand UGX. I used the money toward my education.

The postage stamp I designed.

In 2001 I decided to take a risk and move away from my home to pursue advanced-level secondary education at a school located in a war zone in Northern Uganda. School fees in this region were a lot cheaper, which benefited me. I joined Sacred Heart Girls Boarding Secondary School in Gulu District. This school comprises at least four hundred students. The rebels of the Lord's Resistance Army (LRA) led by Joseph Kony had previously abducted girls from this school. The Uganda People's Defence Force (UPDF) guarded our school, and we had a rule that lights were off by eight o'clock in the evening. During this time the students and the people in this region lived in fear because the rebels were still actively operating. Every evening children and adults left their homes to spend the nights at the veranda of shops, at bus parks, and some in our school store to be safe from the rebels. There was also a rumor that the rebels had planned to return to abduct more girls from my school, so we studied in fear.

I was one of the first students to arrive at the beginning of the school year. The first student I met and introduced myself to, as we settled in, was Lanyero Florence. Florence predicted that I was going to become the school president on the first day of school. I was not at all interested in this position, so I didn't take her words seriously. Normally, the procedure to become a student leader involved interested students applying for various positions and campaigning for them. After a few weeks of campaign, an election was carried out school-wide whereby students voted for their favorite candidates. In my case, I did not show interest or even apply for any position. However, when the list of candidates came out, my name was among the three school presidential candidates. I was resistant and did not actively campaign like other candidates, but surprisingly the students voted me as their leader.

At Sacred Heart Girls Secondary School, the school president also served as the YCS (Young Christian Students Association) section leader. I had no choice but to take up the job. I served the students within the school and represented my school in outside events. Besides overseeing the rest of the student leaders in various capacities, coordinating between the administration and students, and solving students' issues, I made my leadership all about fun for the students.

There were weekly movie nights, dance, and drama in which I actively participated. I also organized events in which I invited students from neighboring schools to attend. I had a different culture and spoke a traditional language different from the people in this region, including 99 percent of the students in my school. To make it more fun, I taught them new songs and fun activities from my culture. I was and had been an aspirant of the Comboni Missionary Sisters since 1997. The students in my new school nicknamed me "Sister Act" after the movie *Sister Act*. Many of them were inspired by me and became aspirants of Comboni Missionary Sisters as well. As it turned out, the students seemed to have enjoyed my leadership.

I sat for my advanced-level certificate of education at the end of 2002. I performed well but did not make it on government sponsorship. To qualify for government sponsorship to pursue a university degree, a student must meet a certain grade level. Otherwise, they can only join the university on self or private sponsorship.

After graduating advanced-level secondary education, I visited my childhood friend Enid, whom I'd known while living with my father in the city. Her father late Mr. Martin Fetaa was my father's best friend, and he was known to me as an uncle. This family welcomed me and took me in as one of their own.

Their hospitality enabled me to apply to the university to pursue a bachelor's degree in industrial and fine arts. I took the risk to apply without knowing where the tuition would come from; I was accepted. Luckily by this time, my stepmother had begun receiving my father's pension, and she could contribute toward my tuition. I also received extra tuition assistance each semester from a nun who headed a school for disabled children; she saved some of the money she received from sponsors to help me.

Although I couldn't afford all the expensive art materials required for my education, I did all I could to ensure I made it. I still remember a relative I ran into on campus challenging me;

she thought it was a joke that I was a university student. She boldly asked me what I was doing on campus and how I was going to afford it because of my parents' financial situation. I had no words for her. The good news was I made it and earned my bachelor's degree in industrial and fine arts. The family that took me in hosted me throughout my years at the university. I am forever grateful to them.

Two

The Pressure of Cultural Expectations

I am from the Lugbara tribal group of Arua, located in the West Nile region of northern Uganda. In my local language, the word "girl" (*za-mva*) means meat-child, and "boy" (*agu-pia-mva*) means the people's child. In the past only boys were encouraged to attend school, while girls were expected to stay at home, complete domestic work, and get married. Girls were a source of wealth in my culture. When they married, their husband's families were expected to pay a dowry in the form of cows, goats, chicken, and cash to her family.

In the present day, the higher educated a girl is, the higher the number of cows her family would demand from the man who chose to marry her. Now that girls attend school, the pressure is that once they were done with that, the expectation that would earn her and her family respect and praise would be then for her to traditionally introduce a man to marry. During this introduction elders from both families would negotiate how many cows, goats, and chickens and how much money should be given to the girl's family to allow her to marry the man. Once an agreement was made, the man paid the dowry, and he was handed a wife. Both families would celebrate together.

Three

MANY ARE CALLED BUT FEW CHOSEN

While growing up I never wanted to get married. My initial goal in life was to become a nun. As a little girl, I admired religious sisters and dreamed of becoming one in my adulthood. As such, during my secondary school education from 1997 through 2002, I aspired with the Comboni Missionary Sisters. My vocation directresses visited me at school, and I attended orientations during school breaks. While studying in Northern Uganda, I spent most of my short breaks at the convent with the Little Sisters of Mary Immaculate, where my cousin, who was also a nun, resided. I was supposed to begin my journey of pursuing my vocation as a nun right after completing higher secondary school education. However, my cousin who mentored me convinced me to give it all up and further my education instead. Three of my first cousins had already followed the religious path—two became nuns, and one became a priest. Although I did not follow through with my vocation, my aspiration kept me away from the dating scene and allowed me to stay a virgin throughout my teenage years through early twenties.

It also taught me good morals and saved me from some of the common mistakes teenagers made.

In 2003 I joined Makerere University in Uganda and fell in love deeply for the very first time with a boy I met at the university. I envisioned my future with him and felt on top of the world knowing I had found love. But unfortunately the relationship suddenly ended in unexpected breakup during my final year. It was my first painful heartbreak. Moving on was very difficult even when I tried to. I cried so much and never stopped thinking about him. He moved on, and I was still hoping that we could get back together. I would later learn that his new relationship didn't work out, and I still hoped to get back with him, although most of my friends discouraged me.

Four

Unexpected Visitor

One evening while alone in my hostel room, I was thinking about my ex-boyfriend and decided to take out his picture, which I had stored away in my suitcase. I was staring at it while thinking about him and wondering whether I should or shouldn't dial his number.

A knock sounded at my door; it was an unexpected visitor. A guy I had known on campus said he had brought me good news. I invited him in and listened to what he had to tell me. He said he was there to introduce me to a relative of his who liked me and wanted to get to know me better. My new admirer was of the same tribe as me, was well educated, and was pursuing a master's degree abroad in the United States. He had given him my cell phone number, and I was to expect a call from him soon. At that moment I didn't know what to make of the story. I thought it was all a joke and laughed it off, but he insisted that I would be the luckiest girl because he was a good guy.

Five

THE PHONE CALL

The following evening I received a call from an international number. Right away I knew it was the man I had been told about. To me this news coming at a time when I was about to call my ex to reconcile meant it was a sign that I wasn't meant to be with my ex.

Gregory was very soft spoken and spoke in my local language. He told me about himself and the family he came from, which was all familiar to me. His aunt was married to the popular Anglican bishop of our region. Talking to him presented an image of a man any educated woman of my cultural background would want. He was my tribemate and related to a family that was known. He was also highly educated and sounded respectable over the phone, which piqued my interest. I told him about myself and the family I came from as well. We exchanged e-mail addresses and kept in touch from that day forward.

Greg had just completed his master's degree, and he had been accepted to a PhD program within the same university in the United States. He called me at least once every day. We exchanged pictures via e-mail. Our relationship seemed to spiral as we continued to communicate each day. The reason he gave for looking for a bride back home was because his family wanted him to marry a girl from the same tribe. Within the first few weeks of our communication, I would get to meet his aunt's family that lived within the city. Shortly after my graduation, I also met his brother and cousins, who took me to their village to meet the rest of his family.

He began making plans for me to join him in the United States even though we had never met. I was a little hesitant and insisted on meeting him first. He made plans and flew to Uganda on December 15, 2006. His aunt and her husband accompanied me to the airport to meet him for the very first time.

Six

Court and Traditional Marriage

When I realized how serious Greg was, I had to inform my family about him. Usually what they considered to be more important was the man's family background. In Gregory's case, it wasn't that much of a problem because he was related to the popular US-based Anglican bishop's wife. Also a woman from our neighboring clan was married to his uncle, and she convinced my family that he came from a good family. This made it easy for the elders from my clan to welcome those from his clan when they came to ask for my hand in marriage.

A day after his arrival, we traveled to our hometown together. The following day he met my family. After that, we went to Kuluva Hospital in Arua to be tested for HIV. Both results came out negative. That night he proposed—I said yes. While still in the United States, he had suggested that we needed to obtain a marriage certificate from our local court for visa purposes because it might be required. So on December 19, 2006, just three days after we met, we got married in court. The following week the traditional marriage followed, where by elders from his clan met with those from my clan. They negotiated all afternoon and evening as to how much dowry he would pay to my side of the family. I was not allowed to be present during this negotiation or even voice my opinion. Neither my father nor my mother would have a say. It was upon the clan elders to make all decisions. In the end they agreed upon nine cows, some goats, some chickens, traditional wear for my parents, and some money, which was partly paid immediately. The rest would be paid later. I was handed to Greg in front of the crowed, and people feasted and danced all night. The following morning a group of aunties from my village including my great aunts held a meeting in which they lectured me on how to be the perfect traditional wife. They emphasized I should stay obedient and submissive to my husband.

After the traditional marriage, my husband and I traveled to the city to process my visa to the United States. My visa interview was quick. I wasn't asked a lot of questions, neither was I required to provide a marriage certificate. My husband was on a five-year J-1 student visa, hence I was granted a five-year J-2 student dependent visa as well. He bought my airplane ticket to travel right away, so I didn't get to travel back to the village to say good-bye to my family and friends. He left a day before me so he could plan for my arrival. I took my flight the following day. My flight would land in Newark, New Jersey, but my destination with the address I was provided was in Syracuse, New York. I had no clue how far Syracuse would be from New Jersey, and all I had was a hundred-dollar bill and two cell phone numbers to call when I arrived.

It was early January 2007. I had never been abroad, so I was poorly dressed for the winter. I arrived on January 13, 2007. I expected someone to be there at the airport to pick me up, so I waited in the parking lot in freezing cold weather. Hours passed, and no one showed up. I didn't have coins to use to make calls using the pay phones available at the airport. All I had was the hundred-dollar bill, so I walked around and begged for change, which few would give me. A few people freely gave me quarters to use, but unfortunately both numbers went to voicemail, which took my coins. I was left to beg all over again.

I wasn't sure how the voicemail system operated—our phones back home didn't work like that—so I didn't leave any messages. I didn't personally know the people I was calling, so it was a little difficult. I was shivering from spending long hours outside in the cold, and people stared at me awkwardly. I was also becoming speech impaired from the cold. I wanted to take a cab to Syracuse, but I was unaware of the distance from New Jersey. Somehow my instincts also held me back. I would later discover that Syracuse would be more than four hours away from New Jersey.

It was around seven o'clock in the evening when an airport guard, a West African, approached me and invited me inside to keep warm. He decided to stay with me and continuously call the numbers I had with his personal cell phone. Thankfully, a few minutes later, one of the numbers went through, and there was an answer. I introduced myself.

The lady on the other side of the phone responded, "Oh my God...oh my God...oh my God." She promised to be there in an hour's time. She lived in Poughkeepsie, New York, and she would bring me to her home.

Gregory arrived that night with a rose for me. He said his flight was delayed at Amsterdam. I was happy he was finally there. The following day his officemate and his friend, a Ugandan student, drove us to Syracuse. On arrival I overheard them tell my husband not to take me to his place. The Ugandan student offered to sacrifice his apartment for us until my husband found an apartment of his own, but Greg declined his offer.

I had no idea why they wouldn't want him to take me to his place—until we arrived where we were supposed to be living. It was an abandoned house in a neighborhood where one would rarely see people. Another Ugandan who flipped houses (bought old houses, renovated them, and resold them) owned the house Gregory was living in this house for free on an arrangement that he sold flowers for its owner.

The house smelled of rotten wood; it had muddy, dirty stuff all over. Greg only used one of the bedrooms upstairs, which he heated using a space heater. To get to his room, I had to maneuver my way through stinky, dirty floors and stuff. The water in the pipes and toilets was frozen. We took half baths in a freezing cold bathroom using purchased water that we heated with an electrical jar, filled in a basin, and carried to the bathroom. We used our hands to sprinkle it over our bodies. Whatever business we needed to do in the toilet stayed on top of the frozen water since the toilet couldn't flush.

Greg went to school every morning while I stayed locked up in this room until evening. He instructed me never to open the door for anyone who knocked because he didn't trust the owner of the home. Every evening we went out to get food that we ate on disposable plates. Despite our living conditions, he ensured I had something to snack on while he was away. He would also take me to his office a few times so I could call my family. We lived here for two weeks until my husband found a cheap one-bedroom apartment at $380 per month. It was warm and cozy. There was hot water and a kitchen. I could cook. We also had neighbors, and I could see people when I looked out of the window. The people living here were mostly Bosnian immigrants who spoke little or no English. I could relate to them, given I was a foreigner myself. Life finally became normal despite the horrible winter of Syracuse, and I was a happy wife.

Seven

BABY ON BOARD

I would soon find out I was pregnant. It didn't matter to me because we were married and should have been ready to start a family anyway. But Greg was concerned because of how difficult it would be to raise a child here in the United States. I consoled him that all would be fine. His plan was that when our child turned two, we would take him to Uganda for our families to raise.

The first three months of my pregnancy were not easy. I was sick and weak because I vomited every day and had no appetite. What bothered me was my husband's attitude in the beginning. He often said I was pretending to be sick and accused me of putting my finger in my throat to vomit. He compared me to another Ugandan student who was five months pregnant and was not feeling sick as I was. I hadn't received any medical help since I didn't have health insurance, so I was unaware of how long my condition would last. I did not blame him either because we were both first-time parents.

During my second trimester, we decided to seek medical attention at a community hospital. Luckily for me, my midwife was Ruth Ndeze, a South African native. She was very helpful and provided me with all the necessary information I needed. She also helped me to obtain Medicaid and register for WIC—Women, Infants, and Children. Qualifying for Medicaid enabled me to receive health care without paying a penny, and the WIC program provided me with healthy food such as milk, vegetables, juice, cheese, beans, rice, and peanut butter. When my child was born, he also qualified for these services.

Once I started feeling stronger as the symptoms subsided and I was getting medical help, my husband's attitude changed for the better. We went to my doctor appointments together. He often massaged me and took good care of me. Everything seemed fine. We attended international students events together and even actively participated in one traditional cultural presentation. I accompanied him to Canada for a one-day field trip.

I also began attending English-conversation group meetings at the International Students Center at Syracuse University. Since I was fluent in English, our group leader (the teacher) and I became very good friends. Maria picked me up at least once a week to show me places since I was usually alone while my hubby was at school. She introduced me to the women's Bible study group, and sometimes we'd go out to have ice cream or picnics. Somehow my husband didn't like the relationship that was evolving between my teacher and me, and he urged me to be careful. Shortly after that I didn't know what happened, but my friend suddenly stopped communicating.

I was five months pregnant when I started working as a cashier at a convenient store and was earning a minimum wage. I had a student dependent identification, so I took the bus for free to and from work. We opened a checking account in which I would deposit my weekly paystubs.

Right after my arrival in the United States, my husband asked to have the password to my e-mail—I didn't have his. He checked and read my e-mails daily before I did. When I acquired an ATM for my bank account, he also knew the password and oversaw it. When I wanted to purchase anything, I had to ask him first. When monthly statements arrived, he analyzed them. If he saw any charges he was unaware of, such as those I might have used to purchase snack at work, he would yell at me.

He often said, "You will someday remember this money when you return to Uganda."

With his permission I started saving twenty dollars per week in a WIC juice can that I created as a piggy bank. He was also against me telling any member of his family or my family that I was employed. He warned me the day I told a family member that I had started working.

One day we went strolling at the mall as part of my pregnancy exercise. I began feeling pain in my lower back. I found it difficult to move when we arrived home, so I requested my husband's help to serve us dinner. He got so angry and told me he was pregnant too and experienced each and everything I experienced. He added that he was not stupid to have kept quiet about his feelings. I never answered him, but I was moody and went to take a shower. When I got out of the shower, he was on phone with his aunt and her husband, who reside in California. He told them that we were not living on good terms. He stated that I had developed an attitude because he didn't have money. They asked to speak with me and advised me to be the kind of wife "who puts bread on the table." They also told him that my unpleasant behaviors could be due to pregnancy.

Later that night when I questioned Greg why he would say the things he said about me, his explanation was that his aunt's husband owed him money, and he wanted them to pay him back, but he didn't know how to ask them. I was disappointed that he would give his relatives that kind of image about me, but I let it go.

Eight

LIVING WITH A STRANGER

Right from the beginning of our arrival in the United States and living together as husband and wife, I noticed my husband was on regular medication. I had no knowledge about these prescription medications and did not know why he took them. When I asked him why he took them, his response often was to have a good sleep. It didn't really bother me or raise any red flags. I was just living my life and being the kind of wife I was expected to be per our culture. We didn't have a house phone, and I didn't have a cell phone of my own, so I used his cell phone in his presence whenever I needed to speak with my family.

Gregory kept the secret of his depression history and mental illness from me and tried hard to make sure I didn't find out by treating me a certain way. He was very controlling and never allowed me to have a cell phone the entire time of us living together. I had no friends except those he introduced to me, and he was often bitter about female friends I met on my own. The controlling and psychologically abusive behavior worsened when he realized that I had found out about his mental health issues through the friend he introduced to me and through a phone conversation I had with my family. They had learned from sources back home that he was mentally ill and were concerned for my well-being. Since I didn't have a cell phone and spoke to my family only occasionally in his presence using his cell phone, there was no privacy.

One day I called home in his presence as usual. Over the phone my brother expressed the family's concern about my well-being. They were worried about me and needed to know if I was okay. My stepmother, who was a Ford Foundation Scholar, the same as my husband, had found out from their scholarship office that my husband suffered from mental illness. My brother was questioning me over the phone if I was aware of that and okay.

My husband had given me a different version of something that happened to him in 2003. According to him, he was homesick and had to return to Uganda for a whole year before he returned to complete his studies. I explained to my brother his version of the story and assured him that whatever they had heard was a lie and that we were living happily and didn't have any issues.

After getting off the phone, my husband just mumbled in my local language, "They could be right." But he was visibly either hurt or disappointed.

I encouraged and assured him that whatever it was, we would get through it, and I would always stand by him. My only weakness was openness. I never kept any secrets from him. I trusted him too much, yet he never trusted me. He often twisted anything I told him. At this point I still hadn't realized that he was keeping me from discovering the truth. This rumor having come from my stepmother also made me think she wanted to ruin my marriage. I was angry with both my brother and stepmother. I called her and asked her to apologize to my husband. I also e-mailed my brother to dismiss whatever he had heard and convince him that my hubby was fine and a good guy. My brother apologized and promised me that no one would ever know.

One of the few people my husband introduced to me when I arrived in the United States was a Ugandan lady who was his former professor and a PhD student at the same university as my husband. She and I became friends; we were both pregnant at that time. She didn't have a car, so she would ride with us to the grocery store sometimes.

Something strange I noticed about her was that she often got scared if Greg drove carelessly or seemed moody. She would ask me if he was okay and taking his medication. I was clueless when she asked such questions. One day while she and I were alone, she told me my husband suffered from some form of mental illness. She said he was supposed to be taking his medication.

I didn't believe her either. Like my brother and stepmother, I thought she was just against my marriage. Instead I gave her his version of the story and dismissed what she said as something false. I never wanted to believe anything these people said, plus my husband never opened up to me about it, so it was often difficult even to bring it up. The only visible signs I could notice then were that he was often forgetful and seemed slow or moody sometimes. But it was never a big deal to me. The truth according to one of his relatives was that back in 2003, he got into a bus going to Buffalo, New York, from Syracuse. Police officers there found him in a state in which he could not say his name. He was taken to the hospital and after sent back to Uganda for a year before he could return to the United States to complete his studies.

I was eight months pregnant when I began seeing a stranger side of my husband. One day he brought home unfamiliar greens from the farmer's market that I couldn't prepare because I did not know what they were. He prepared the greens himself and called it "*osubi*," a local kind of greens in our culture. He also put lots of spices in it. The day he prepared it, it tasted fair, but the next day it tasted horrible, as if a lot of salt had been added to it. Since my husband and I had started living together as husband and wife, for unknown reasons to me he never let me eat off my own plate when it was just him and me. We ate from the same plate the entire time of us living together whenever I cooked. So when these greens tasted badly the following evening as we ate dinner, I suggested to him that we shouldn't eat it. He quickly poured his drinking water into the bowl containing the greens and drank it. Later he had a bottle of beer before we went to bed.

The following day, his cousin—the lady who had picked me up from the airport—came to Syracuse with a couple of her Ugandan friends to throw a surprise baby shower for me. My husband's friends—fellow African community members and some classmates of his—were also invited. I had no clue this surprise party was being organized. However, Gregory didn't seem himself this specific day. During the baby shower, his cousin somehow noticed and asked him if he was okay. His response was that he drank something the previous night that was affecting his head. When we got home after the baby shower, I asked him jokingly if the one bottle of beer he drank the previous night still affected him, as he had told his cousin.

It was as if my husband had been waiting to explode. He got angry and accused me of poisoning his food. I had never seen him that angry. He claimed I had been poisoning his food this whole time to damage his brain. He said the fact that he kept quiet about things didn't mean he didn't know what was going on around him. I was in total shock and couldn't believe what I had just heard. He went on to force me to sit in front of him and eat the leftovers of the same dish that was still in the fridge to prove to him that I hadn't poisoned the food. He said he wanted to see what was going to happen to me. In tears and in disbelief, I ate this horrible-tasting food. Nothing happened to me or our unborn baby.

After this night, I wasn't myself. I worried so much and spent at least two weeks feeling stressed out. I became kind of scared of him and wrote him a letter explaining that I would never in my life do anything of that nature. I was not the evil person whom he thought I was. Gregory apologized and explained to me that he used to live with Indians who put stuff in his food to make him sick, and he thought I was doing the same. I then begged him never ever to falsely accuse me again. I forgave him.

After our son Ethan was born, I still didn't have a cell phone or a house phone, but we had Internet at home, so Greg and I communicated through Yahoo Messenger if we needed to communicate while he was at school. One day he messaged me and stated that if he didn't make it home by nine o'clock that evening, then something must have happened to him. He explained that he had taken coffee, and it seemed someone put something in it, and it was badly affecting his head. I begged him to hurry home. He did make it home safely, but he complained of a headache and went to sleep.

On a different day within the same time frame, Gregory worked late on the computer one night while the baby and I went to bed before him. He went to bed late and woke up early before me. When he reached school, he realized his flash drive was missing. He messaged me to check for it around the computer, but I couldn't find it. This turned out to be hell for me again when he returned home. He claimed I hid his flash drive because I was not happy with his education. It was such a painful accusation to hear from my spouse. I cried to him that I didn't do it, but he didn't listen to me. He later found it in his pajama pocket. It seemed as though I didn't know my husband anymore as things continued to take a different turn.

After our baby was born, I needed a babysitter so I could continue to work. One day on the bus on my way home from work, I met a Congolese lady whose husband was also a PhD student at Syracuse University. We all happened to be living in the same apartment complex. I learned from Tatiana that she was unemployed and would be willing to babysit for me. Since I needed a babysitter badly, I told my husband about her; he supported the idea. A few days later, we met my new friend and her husband, who both then became our friends. Tatiana started babysitting for us, and I would pay her weekly.

In March 2008, there was an incident. Gregory had, a few months prior, crashed his car, and so both doors on the passenger side couldn't open. He claimed he called the police after the crash, but no one showed up. This car had also begun having several other mechanical issues, making us spend lots of money on it. One day I suggested that we sell it off and buy another one—a secondhand car that we could find in a catalog I had seen at my workplace. He said no one would buy our car at a higher price than $500 because of its condition, but I suggested we try the dealers.

Luckily enough, the dealer we went agreed to take it for $2,000, but he told us to come back the next day. Greg was very excited, so he cleaned the car and took it for an oil change at Walmart while I went to work that day. I worked two jobs—as a cashier at a convenient store and as a food service worker at upstate medical university hospital cafeteria where my work schedule was five o'clock in the evening to eleven o'clock. He was supposed to pick me up at eleven that night. At around ten o'clock, I called Greg on my lady coworker's phone to tell him he didn't have to bring the baby out in the cold because the lady whose phone I used had offered to give me a ride home. I had asked for a ride from her because I was concerned for our five-month-old baby's health; a couple of days prior, Gregory had locked the car with the house keys in it after picking the baby from the sitter, so they couldn't get into the house. He had stayed with the baby in the cold, and I was worried that the baby might get sick.

Unaware of how Greg's day had gone, I called him using my coworker's cell phone. To my surprise he answered the call and began yelling at me over the phone in our local language, accusing me of planning to murder him.

He continued to yell, "Why do you want to kill me? Why do you want to kill me?" Then he hung up without any explanations.

I was confused and shaking. When I called him back several times, he never picked up, but I left messages pleading with him to tell me what was going on. I was shaking and wanted to leave work, but my coworker helped me calm down.

At around ten thirty, he called back and asked me to go pick him up from Walmart with the lady who was supposed to give me a ride. It was after picking him up that he explained what had happened. On his way back from getting the oil changed, the car broke down on the highway. The cops who showed up on the scene told him the person who changed the oil most likely forgot to replace it.

As soon as my coworker dropped us off, he changed from being calm to a whole different person. While we stopped at the babysitter's apartment to pick up the baby, he accused me of planning with people around him to kill him. He said my reason for calling him that night was to confirm if he was already dead—because per him I already knew he was supposed to crash in a car accident and die and I was behind it all. He believed I planned with Walmart to murder him. He continued to accuse me in front of the babysitter and her husband, stating that I was poisoning his food because every time he ate he developed headaches, yet we both often ate from the same plate. I was so devastated, confused, and embarrassed that I didn't even know how to defend myself.

When we got home, he didn't stop. He continued to accuse me that he knew about all my plans and attempts to kill him. He said I had also planned with National Grid—the electric company—to kill him because according to him, it was unusual that they were offering us discounts on our electric bill. In the past representatives from the electric company had stopped by our door to market. Since our electric bill was in Gregory's name, I gave them his number so they could talk to him directly because he wasn't home that day.

Greg didn't sit down or even stop talking when we got home. He was moving up and down within the house. I had never seen him in that state before. I figured something must be wrong with him and tried to calm him, but instead he threatened me to move out of his sight and not say a word before he lost his temper and did something bad to me.

Something within me told me to take the baby and run. I waited for him to walk toward the bedroom. I grabbed the baby and his phone and ran out of the house in the cold about half a mile to Remington Apartments, where a Ghanaian family lived. I knocked at their door and cried for help, but no one opened. I then decided to call his aunt in California to let her know what was going on. She instructed me to call the police right away, and so I did.

Two police officers picked the baby and me up. I confirmed to them that Gregory didn't have any weapons, and so they took us back home. While at our apartment, the police asked to see Greg's medication. They discovered he wasn't seeing his doctor anymore and had not been taking his medication. He told them he had unpaid bills and no medical insurance to see his doctor. He also told the cops that I was a witch.

The police advised me to leave and stay somewhere with a friend or relative, but I declined. I told them I would be okay. They proceeded to take him to the hospital, where he spent the night and part of the day seeing a counselor, who kept in touch with me for that period. Upon his release from the hospital, he later told his classmate who picked him up that I had done a wise thing although he never stopped blaming me for involving the cops.

After he was released from the hospital, I decided that we would open the juice can in which I had been saving twenty dollars weekly to see how much we had; maybe we could use some of that money toward a secondhand car. To our surprise I had saved about $2,500 in the juice can. I had brought home a used-car catalog from work in which we located and bought a used car at this price. Gregory was happy, and he praised me for being a good wife. He later sued Walmart as the cops had instructed him when his car broke down after oil change, and he won about $2,000 from Walmart.

After we purchased the car, I decided that we register this car in both of our names. Gregory was a little hesitant, but he later agreed. While at the Department of Motor Vehicles, we encountered another problem that would make me discover something else about Greg. This was not very shocking to me, but it shed more light to an issue I had encountered earlier on in our relationship and shortly before coming to United States. The DMV wouldn't allow him to add me as a co-owner because he already had two cars registered in his name and another woman's name, and their insurance had lapsed. He was to pay $500 before they could reinstate everything.

Mellissa was the woman whose relationship with Gregory I did not completely understand. While still in Uganda, I had text messaged Greg, but a woman responded basically threatening me that Gregory was her man, and he had spent the night at her house and had left his phone with her. She wanted me to call her so she could tell me more, but I never responded to her.

After receiving her messages, I decided to break things off with Gregory over the phone when he called me. I clearly explained to him that I didn't want to come to a foreign country and suffer. I also told him I did not want to come between him and this woman. He claimed this woman was nothing to him. She was Ghanaian and a US citizen by birth who he wanted to marry to acquire US citizenship. He also added that it was something she did for money. He said his family wanted him to marry a woman from home, and they would never allow him to be with her. He described her as a crazy person who just liked to mess around with him.

Over several days Greg had two of his Ugandan colleagues call me just to convince me that everything was going to be okay and insist that this woman was not in his life. They also insisted that I would be safe if I joined him in the United States. Gregory even stated that he had been crying ever since the woman threatened me and that was why his friends intervened. After speaking with Joseph and John, I believed Gregory and decided to move on with the relationship. But after coming to the United States, I came to realize that both still did some things together.

One day Gregory had issues with his car insurance, and he happened to be talking to his Ugandan colleague about it. The Ugandan guy asked him how much he paid for auto insurance in my presence. Greg mentioned that they had two cars registered in his name and Mellissa's, and so insurance had to be paid for both cars. Later when I hadn't asked him, he felt guilty and explained to me that paying Mellissa's car insurance didn't mean anything. He promised to cancel it right away, but this went on for a whole year until between January and February 2008 when he couldn't afford to pay for both cars. The insurance lapsed, and the DMV wouldn't allow him to register our car in both of our names.

I would later learn from his colleague and relative here in the United States that this woman was a student on whom Gregory spent a lot of money and who seemed to use him for her benefit. I also learned that she dropped him off at the airport when he traveled to Uganda to meet me and bring me along to the United States. I just didn't understand whether he continued to financially support her during our marriage.

Nine

TROUBLE WITH THE LAW

When our son was seven months old, we got into a little trouble with the law for leaving him in the car at a Chinese buffet. We had been very busy shopping and traveling from one store to another that day. We decided to get Chinese food from a buffet since it was going to be late to prepare dinner that evening. The baby had fallen asleep when we got there, so we decided not to take him out of the car. Greg went in to serve us dinner while I stayed in the car with the baby. At some point I exited the car briefly to go tell him what to serve me and return to the car right away. We left shortly after.

A few minutes after arriving home, there was a knock on our door. It was two police officers who wanted to know if we had been to the Chinese buffet and left a baby in the car. I admitted to them that we were there and did leave the baby in the car but briefly. I explained to them that our car was still running, and we had the hazard lights flashing, since I was only gone for a short time. I also told them that we were new to the country and didn't know that it was against the law to do so. The officers gave us a warning never to do it again and left. The following morning while Gregory was at school, a lady from child protective services showed up at our door. She asked me questions about the incident at the restaurant. She also asked to see where our baby slept and check if we had food for him. I led her to our bedroom and showed her the crib and then to the kitchen to see all the food we had stocked for the baby. She took our babysitter's information and told me that they would investigate us for sixty days. After the sixty days passed, we received a letter stating that the case was unfounded and dismissed.

Ten

Helpless in a Foreign Land

I went through extreme psychological abuse in Gregory's hands. I believe he never totally understood how much pain and torture it was causing me. I had no people I could talk to apart from his aunt and uncle, whom I'd never physically met. I had lost so much weight and even feared climbing on the scale because what I weighed at some point was under my usual more than 110 pounds. His aunt and uncle advised me not to seek help through legal authorities except through a church to prevent my husband from getting in any trouble. His aunt was very helpful. She secretly told me to call her whenever I was at work so I could openly tell her the things that were happening. At this point they had begun opening up to me about his mental health issues, advising me to ensure he took his medication. But Greg still never freely talked to me about it, so I was often afraid to bring it up. His aunt strongly supported me from a distance. She once told me if my death occurred due to my husband's mental illness, then there would be no case; she emphasized I take care of myself.

Gregory was so insecure that he believed nobody liked him or our son. He made accusations against me, such as planning with doctors to kill our baby. Whenever there were doctor appointments and delays to see the baby, he would claim the delays were intentional because it was his child and no one in America liked him. He accused me and the doctors of giving the baby growth hormones because our son was tall while he, as the father, was shorter. I was taller than him, and my son must've taken the genes from my side of the family, but Greg never understood it. This was a disturbing problem for me.

One day our family friend, the Ugandan PhD student, invited us and other guests to her home for dinner. When we arrived at her home, the baby had fallen asleep. I took him out of the car seat, held him in my arms, and walked into her apartment ahead of Gregory. As soon as I walked in, Susan, the owner of the home, welcomed us in and asked me to lay the baby down in her son's crib so he could sleep comfortably and my hands could be free. Gregory didn't like that I wasn't holding the baby. When we got home, he confronted me about it and claimed I did that to hide our baby away from the guests because our baby was ugly. He often didn't like it when I spoke to other people during such gatherings. He complained that I didn't call him honey when his friends were around.

On another occasion we went to Boston, Massachusetts, for the Uganda Martyrs celebration. Lots of Ugandan people were there from Syracuse, Poughkeepsie, and Boston. His cousin— the lady who had picked me up from the airport—was also there with her family. The men were hanging out together, and so were the ladies. I decided to join the ladies group since it was obvious the men were together, and the women who were the spouses of these men had also gathered together in a group.

Gregory was angry that I left him with the guys and joined the women. He confronted me about it, and I was really shocked. The ladies I was associating with were the wives and girlfriends of the men he was hanging out with, so I at this point just didn't know what to expect of him. It was as though I was getting in trouble for the simplest things.

I was psychologically disturbed to the point that I was beginning to believe that maybe everyone else viewed me the same way my husband viewed me, that is, as an evil person. I was so afraid to talk about it with anyone because I believed if I mentioned to them the things my husband had accused me of, they wouldn't want to talk to me ever again and would view me as an evil person as well. So I kept it all to myself, although I was feeling extremely disturbed, and the pain was eating me up.

I had been very open and honest with my husband from the very beginning. He had known passwords and details of my credit card and my e-mail address. He checked and read my e-mails and could ask for my debit card to shop, put gas in the car, or withdraw money anytime, and I never refused him to do so at any point. He often opened my mail, calculated and analyzed my bank statements, and closely monitored how money was spent. What bothered me was I never sent my family money or supported them in any way because I was working toward the well-being of the three of us (child, husband, and wife), and yet he was controlling my entire world as though I had built a secret mansion somewhere. I never felt any freedom even to spend the money I worked hard for. I worked more than forty hours a week and sometimes felt hungry at work. I would buy something to eat, spending a dollar or two, but I got in trouble when this money reflected on my bank statement. He even told me to stop buying stuff to eat at work. I many times stayed hungry at work simply because I was afraid if I used my card to buy something or even withdrew money it would show in my bank statement, and I would get in trouble.

I never bought myself anything in Gregory's absence. Like I said before, I often had to ask his permission first or we shopped together. During one of those shopping trips, I purchased myself underwear. One night when I had my new underwear on, my husband started questioning me frantically, asking who bought me the underwear I was wearing. I was shaken and shocked! But I kept my composure and explained to him when and where we bought the underwear. After some time he figured it out and laughed about it, although it wasn't funny at all given he was very serious about it.

On a different night, Gregory confiscated my debit card out of the blue and said he was going to wire all the money to his brother's account in Uganda. He claimed I did not need any money. He also logged onto the computer and said he was going to use it to buy phones from the Internet to send to Uganda. I did not understand why he decided to treat me like that. I knelt in front of him and pleaded with him to have my card back. Despite my plea and cry, he refused to surrender it. He said I could call the police or his aunt in California if I wanted—he didn't care. He kept me awake all night until late that morning, yet I had to be at work by seven thirty that morning. I was extremely stressed and continued to lose weight.

With all that I was going through, there were moments I felt so tired and didn't feel desire for sex and told Greg so, but he got angry at me, stating I was his wife and always must be ready for sex whenever he wanted it. To avoid further issues, I would let him proceed and do his act even though it wasn't pleasuring to me. I never really opened up to anyone, not even my friend Susan, the PhD student, about the things I was going through. But somehow people seemed to figure things out for themselves.

One day another Ugandan student, the niece to the man who flipped houses (the owner of the house without heat or hot water that we lived in), came to my house to have her hair done. She was not really my friend or one of the people I talked to on regular basis. This day as I did her hair, she started telling me some details about my husband's mental illness that I didn't know. She advised me to start saving money just in case.

All these revelations coming from outsiders made me realize what a stranger I was in my own home and what more I didn't know that was yet to strike.

Early September 2008 the lady from Poughkeepsie invited us for her son's birthday celebration. We had come to Poughkeepsie from Syracuse, and several Ugandans attended this function. I had lost so much weight that during the gathering, I could hear people gossiping. I did not exactly know what they were saying, but I could sense that they were talking about me. My suspicions were confirmed after we returned to Syracuse. The lady who hosted called my husband, asking him questions and demanding to know what was going on between us because I didn't look myself. People had noticed that something was wrong, and they were concerned. My husband told her to call me on Skype and ask me herself, which she did. Thankfully my husband was not home when she called, so I was able to open up to her about some of the issues I was going through. She then requested John, the Ugandan student and a friend of hers as well as my husband, to keep checking on me.

It was after talking to her that I began gaining the strength to stand up for myself. Most of my fears were from our cultural background. I wanted to be the perfect traditional wife. I knew separating from my husband would cause me a lot of trouble, given dowry was involved. It would bring shame to me and my family. Some women had been sent back to their husbands, especially if dowry was involved. It didn't matter whether the husband was abusive or not; the wife had to submit to him.

I didn't want to be the woman to be gossiped about, given he brought me to America and people would judge me for leaving him. I had wanted to stick with my husband no matter what, but somehow the psychological torture had become unbearable. The most hurtful part of it all was my husband often suspecting me of being one capable of planning his murder. How could I live comfortably with my spouse who believed I was poisoning his food and couldn't even eat off his own plate? As I ate food every day, these accusations would play in my head, and I'd feel more hurt. I felt so helpless and began falling out of love, but I remained faithful.

Eleven

THE ESCAPE

When my friend Susan graduated with her PhD and was preparing to return to Uganda, she decided to leave her cell phone for me to use for emergency purposes. Since my husband was against me owning a phone, I offered to pay bills for both of our phones so he could at least give me the freedom to have access to a cell phone. He agreed, but after Susan left, he was against the idea of me having a phone.

Late September 2008 Greg tried to get me to drink alcohol, which I refused. Later the same night, he called Sprint to cancel both phone lines for no reason. He came into the bedroom while I was putting the baby to sleep and lay on top of me, demanding sex—stating I had to even if I wanted it or not. I had lost so much weight by then, and he weighed a lot more than I did. I pleaded with him to let me put the baby to bed first, but he wouldn't stop pressing his body against mine. He got very angry because I was resisting him. He accused me of being responsible for deaths of people in my clan, stating he didn't even know who I was. He was verbally aggressive and threw the bedsheets and blankets on me.

Seeing him in that state, I tried to calm him by talking to him nicely. But he threatened me to get out of his sight before he hurt me while he walked around the house. He said that he was going to buy coffins to take dead bodies home to Uganda. I instinctively figured things were taking a turn for the worst—he sounded suicidal.

I feared for my life, so I grabbed the baby and the phone with hopes it was still on and ran out of the house in the middle of the night. I couldn't go to the babysitter's house because I knew he would figure I was there, so I called John, the Ugandan PhD student (the one who drove us to Syracuse from Poughkeepsie when I arrived from Uganda), to hurry and pick us up before Greg found us. I also called his aunt and her husband to inform them of what was going on. While at John's I didn't know what was happening to me, but I couldn't breathe. John had to put me outside on his balcony to recover while he cared for my baby.

Although the baby and I were already safe, Greg's aunt advised me to call 911 for his own safety, which I did. The cops took him to the hospital. Meanwhile his aunt suggested I move to Poughkeepsie to live with their relative temporarily. She told me they would trick him into believing that I was only going away for a few weeks' break so he would allow me to leave. But the plan was for me to leave for good.

The following morning John and Greg's colleague accompanied me to our apartment to get my purse and a diaper for the baby. They then dropped me and the baby off at the train station, where I took the train to Poughkeepsie. I was so afraid of my husband that I didn't even pack myself or the baby any belongings. All I ensured I had was my debit card. I quit my job, and since then I never returned to our marital home. He deliberately refused to support us financially and even refused to provide medical insurance for our son, demanding if I needed him to do so I must return. I applied for Medicaid for my son, but it was denied because out of fear I declined to file for child support. Thankfully after a month of being unemployed, I got a job and could acquire health care for my child and me.

Twelve

Bad Luck or Karma

I decided to treat myself to a new cell phone after starting my new job. That day my host and I went to the mall shopping for winter clothes for our kids. We stopped at T-Mobile and purchased a BlackBerry flip phone with a new number for me. I also bought insurance for my new phone just in case something happened to it. I hadn't used my phone at all except for a welcome message that came from T-Mobile. I placed the phone in my pocket and left its box in the car as we proceeded to shop at Burlington Coat Factory.

While shopping I saw some African American young men who seemed to be shopping in the area where we were, but there was no reason for us to be suspicious of anything. We got everything we needed, checked out, and left. However, when we arrived home, I could not find my phone. It could still ring when we called it, but no answer. We called Burlington Coat Factory, but no one had seen it. I faulted when I called my phone's insurance before the thirty-day rule and could not get a new phone. The thirty-day rule stated that you can only call to make a claim after thirty days of owning the phone. I should have waited for at least thirty days before calling, but I faulted when I called them sooner. I was told to report the case to the police and acquire some type of number, which I did.

Two weeks later a homicide detective showed up at our door. They had found my phone in the pocket of a dead body, a boy who had been killed in Poughkeepsie. Having reported the loss of my phone to the police earlier saved me from something serious. I explained to him how I had lost the phone and showed him its box, which I still had in my possession. He then told us the victim had a history of theft. He wanted to return the phone to me, but I refused it. He left his business card and left with it. So scary! End of story.

Thirteen

The Intervention

Early October 2008, my husband decided to show up unannounced at the address where I was living in Poughkeepsie. He was speaking aggressively to me and following me throughout the house. When I went to the bathroom, he would follow me and stand by the door while repeating previous accusations he often made about me, including stating I was responsible for his mental illness and have been after him since he was in high school. Of course, I could not have known him during his high-school years.

As this was going on, I didn't say a word to him, and he would not leave me alone. These incidents happened in front of witnesses, causing me extreme emotional distress. My host and her spouse decided to take me away from this address to a different location. As the man who would drive me away from there and I walked toward the car, Gregory was following closely behind me as he continued to speak. I quickly jumped into the passenger side and closed the door. The man who drove had to use back roads to ensure Greg was not following us in his car. He took me to another Ugandan family's home within the Poughkeepsie area, where I spent the rest of that day and night. The next day I returned home, where I had left my child, after I was told he was gone. I would later learn from his cousin that he had suggested that they give me Valium so I could sleep and then they could bring me back to him while I was asleep.

On October 11, 2008, Gregory arrived unannounced at his relative's address in Poughkeepsie where I was living. He kept his bags in my bedroom. But when it was bedtime, his cousin told him to sleep on the couch. At around midnight he began pounding on my locked door using the excuse that he wanted to get his bag. As this was going on, his cousin, who was in the next bedroom, kept in touch with me via phone to ensure I was okay. When he wouldn't stop, she intervened and told me to open the door so he could get his bags. As soon as I opened the door, Greg pushed me back and then locked the door while our child, Ethan, was in the bedroom. He forcefully held my hands, pressing his body against mine on the wall demanding unwanted sex, ignoring his cousin's constant orders to open the door. He stopped upon hearing our child cry hysterically. His cousin made him leave immediately, mentioning she would call police on him if he didn't do so. He left. One of his male relatives, whom I talked to over the phone whenever these incidences occurred, told me to allow him to have intercourse with me so he could feel better. What a shock! I didn't.

On January 2, 2009, Greg showed up unannounced for the third time at the residence where I was living. At eleven o'clock at night he went into my bedroom with our son and locked the door. He refused my repeated request to unlock the door, but he finally opened it. He was sifting through my personal belongings and paperwork, which he had scattered everywhere. He found my diary and became very angry that I was writing about him. An argument ensued. He demanded I leave that house because the owner of the house was not related to me but him.

I was not sure who called the police, but they showed up unexpectedly and made him leave immediately. He told the police that I was dependent on him and could never take care of myself. I was issued a police report and given a brochure of the Battered Women Services and told to contact them for help in the morning. The following morning the Battered Women Services sent a cab to pick me up. They counseled me and helped me through the process of obtaining an order of protection through family court.

I was supposed to move to a shelter right away, but thankfully I had just started a new job as a direct-care professional at the Anderson Center for Autism, so I could afford a one-bedroom apartment at $650 a month for my child and me. I quickly moved into my new apartment, which was kept confidential. The Battered Women Services continued to work with me in the months to come. They supplied me with furniture and all the things I needed for my new apartment, including groceries. They directed me to the other free programs, such as the Legal Services of the Hudson Valley, who helped me obtain a divorce, and the Catholic Charities, which helped me through the process of renewing my legal status in the country.

Fourteen

SATELLITE-ELECTRONIC BRAIN HARASSMENT

In January 2010 I was forwarded an e-mail thread that had been started by my ex-husband. The e-mails had been sent to subscribers of eastafrica@lists.ifponline.org. It was forwarded to me by one of its recipients, who happened to be my family member. The recipients of these e-mails were international students studying here in the United States.

One may wonder why I have chosen to write about this; I didn't have to. However, I wanted to prove a point here due to the many evil things I had been accused of in the past by my ex-husband. To this date, some of his relatives still blame me for leaving him. They failed to understand the psychological torture I went through at the hands of my ex. He never trusted me. He blamed me for his mental illness. He often thought I was poisoning his food. He also thought I had powers to plan with big companies to kill him, yet I was innocent and new to this country. After I left and years had passed, he could not accuse me anymore; instead he believed he was being targeted and harassed by US military surveillance technology.

His e-mail to eastafrica@lists.ifponline.org on Tuesday, January 5, 2010, read as follows:

Subject: Re: Satellite-Electronic brain harassment no longer a secret
Dear,

Has anyone received anonymous electronic harassment—this time not e-mail or junk mails but satellite harassment? For a long time, this has been going on and especially the US military has used the acoustic technology to spy and monitor people and to decode what they are thinking. Acoustic technology uses satellite to scan the brain and to simulate voices from different electronic waves. The effect is not pleasing, it can cause brain damage and loss of memory, induce sleep, and so on. The victims commonly hear voices, like calls from God or close relative or persons you know. The technology can mimic someone's voice play in your brain while you are asleep. For many people this is not new "news" because they have gone through this too many times. I have personally experienced satellite brain distraction for many years now to the extent that even hiding your head under the bed does no good. This is a military surveillance technology; you can read about it in blogs.

Following the same thread as of January 23, 2010, he wrote:

Subject: Re: Satellite-Electronic brain harassment—need help
Fellows;

The science behind this technology is good and was developed for a good purpose. The electronic we use in our daily lives: cell phones, TVs computers, and all those remotely controlled equipment are possible because of this technology. As you know, for every good thing there is also bad part. This is what many activists called brain harassment. Somebody may just pay a large chunk of money to satellite operator to put you out of school for example or in military used for surveillance. So the first thing is to locate those points and tell them to stop. That is the only way. Do I have the ability....no, absolutely no. That was why my first e-mail was copied to those activists who might have the knowledge and can be in better position to stop such kind of act. By broadcasting online maybe some angel or responsible person may do something about it. It is not a scare. It is still none lethal. I think this list serves has already met its fate—several death announcements and did those cause anybody some scare?

His e-mail to the same group of January 23, 2010, read as follows:

Subject: Re: Satellite-Electronic brain harassment—need help
Dear all;

People who have not experienced this kind of thing (Satellite-Electronic brain harassment) would think a message like this is a bull crap! This whole thing undermines our ability to function properly, and we cannot justify our learning experiences when we have this kind of torture. Apparently your cautiousness/experiences will explain whether or not such a thing has happened to you. But I think it is worth noting and telling others that Satellite-Electronic brain harassment is real, and it happens all the time and if not to almost everyone (I mean those who are singled out to be harassed that way). If keeping your mouth "shut" does little or nothing—then let the cat out! I am one!

In the last portion of the e-mail, he added:

Several years have passed, and I can no longer pretend this is happening. Can anyone (███@peaceandprogress.org; ████slavery.org.uk; ████@unorg.ch; eastafrica@███ █online.org) explain how to prevent this kind of attack?

Fifteen

THE WEDDING BUDGET

I left my ex-husband on September 28, 2008. I had not been in touch with him since then, and an active order of protection was in place. Sometime in April 2010, I received two e-mails from him; the subjects were "Proposed Wedding Budget" and "Revised Wedding Budget." In these e-mails he attached a document showing a wedding budget of $32,668 that he had prepared. The documents implied that the two of us were going to be wed, and it was to have people contribute toward our wedding. His message to me read as follows:

> This is a proposed wedding budget. Distribute widely and attach any comments on the side, before I distribute this. I was to come to ████'s for the weekend, but she has declined my visitation. She says she does not know where you stay. I do not know when you are coming back to Syracuse again! You have to settle this now! Because I need to be with Ethan for summer.

He also copied some family members and friends in the e-mail. Of course, there had never been a mention or discussion about any wedding happening between us. I ignored the e-mail, and I believe the rest of the recipients did so as well. I have included a copy of that budget below. Because of my lack of response and active order of protection, I thought this would be the last I heard from Gregory.

PROPOSED WEEDING BUDGET: FOR OFEZU AND DRATERU
PROPOSED CHURCH:
PROPOSED RECEPTION THOUSAND ISLANDS (UNLESS OTHERWISE)

No	Items	Qty	Unit Price in (US $)	Total (US $)
	A. Church and Service			
1	Church fee	1	400	400
2	Engagement rings	2	1200	2400
3	Wedding rings	2	200	400
4	Invitation cards	80	10	800
5	Music rental	1	1,000	1,000
	B. Apparels			
1	Bridal Gowns	1	500	500
2	Changing dress	1	200	200
3	Veil headpiece	2	200	400
4	Gloves	2 pairs	30	60
5	Jewelry (Necklace and ear rings)	2	100	200
6	Shoes	2	100	200
7	Hand bag	1	99	99
8	Bridal flowers	1	250	250
9	Crown	1	50	50
	Shoes	2 pairs	40	80
	C. Groom			
1	Suit	1	300	300
2	Shoes	1	150	150
3	Shirt	2	90	90
4	Belt	2	10	20
5	Neck ties	2	30	30
	Dress	2	20	40
	D. Matron			
1	Dress	1	200	200
2	Hand bag	1	99	99
3	Necklace and ear rings	1	100	100
4	Shoes	1	100	100
	E. Best man			
1	Suit	1	300	300
2	Shoes	1	150	150
3	Shirt	1	90	90
4	Belt	1	30	30
5	Socks	2	10	10
	Neck ties	2	20	40
	F. Maids and Matrons in charge			
1	Dress	4	80	320

Fortunate's Unfortunate Fortunes

	Item	Qty	Unit price	Total
2	Shoes	4	80	320
3	Necklace and ear rings	4	20	80
4	Flowers	4	60	240
G. Flower girls				
1	Dress	2	80	160
2	Shoes	2	30	60
3	Gloves	2	20	40
4	Flowers	2	20	40
5	Body socks	2	20	40
6	Neck lace and Earrings	2	60	120
H. Peg boy				
1	Suit	1	100	100
2	Shoes	1	80	80
3	Shirt	1	60	60
4	Tie	1	20	20
5	Belt	1	20	20
6	Socks	1	20	20
I. Salon				
1	Bridal team	1	400	400
2	Groom team	1	400	400
3	Hankies	2 dozen	80	80
J. Reception				
1	Venue	1	1,000	1,000
2	Tables/ chairs/Tents	unit	500	500
3	Food	unit	2,000	2,000
4	Drinks	unit	2,000	2,000
5	Cake	unit	500	500
6	Staff and gratitude	unit	1,000	1,000
7	Linen and others	unit	200	200
K. Gifts				
1	Attendants	unit	1,000	1,000
2	Bride and Broom	unit	200	200
3	Parents	unit	200	200
4	Other participants	unit	100	100
L. Transportation				
1	Weeding Limos	2	900	1,800
2	Taxis	2	100	200
3	Personal cars	10	50	500
4	Parking	2	100	200
M. Decorations				
1	Flowers	unit	100	100
2	Banquet	unit	200	200
3	Gift wrappers	unit	200	200
4	Ceremony and reception	unit	500	500

	Item	Unit	Unit price	Total
5	cars	unit	200	200
N. Photography				
1	Still and digital	assorted	200	200
2	Video and DVD	1	400	400
3	Album (Digital ans still)	assorted	200	200
O. Publicity and stationary				
1	communication	assorted	200	200
2	Guest book	1	100	100
3	Stationery	assorted	200	200
4	Photocopy and prints	assorted	100	100
P. Music				
1	ceremony		400	400
2	D J reception		500	500
Q. Other expenses				
1	Showers	unit	500	500
2	Rehearsals	unit	500	500
3	Engagement party	unit	500	500
	Bachelors' party	unit	500	500
4	Hotel rooms	unit	300	300
5	Officiant	unit	200	200
6	Security	unit	500	500
7	Cruise Tour	unit	600	600
R. Miscellaneous		2448.8	2068.8	
Grand Total				**US $ 32,668**
The proposed budget is for weeding at the Syracuse, New York				

Note   On average, the weeding costs for couples weeding at Syracuse New york ranges from $33, 238 to $ 55, 394

Part Two

FROM A FRYING PAN INTO THE FIRE

Sixteen

LIFE AS A SINGLE MOTHER

I settled in well as a single mother after escaping Syracuse. It was not totally easy given I was still new to this foreign country. I was working full time and making enough to support my child and me. I worked the second shift from two fifteen in the afternoon till ten fifteen five days a week; my coworkers were basically my family.

I was living in Hyde Park, New York, occupying a top floor of an entire house and had no neighbors. The owner of this house used the bottom floor as a working space and only worked Monday through Friday between eleven in the morning and five in the afternoon. Every weekend and every night, it was just me and my son.

My son's day care was in Fishkill, New York, and I worked in Staatsburg. On working days I would drop him off at Fishkill and drive to work at Staatsburg. After work I would head out to pick him up, and by the time I made it home in Hyde Park, it would be about midnight. This commute was even more hectic on snowy days during winter, but we were surviving. I had purchased my very first personal used car, a 2000 Chrysler Concorde, for $2,000 from a mechanic. It was in great shape and helpful for at least the first two years. However, being a person who didn't know much about cars with no one to tell me of services that needed to be done regularly, such as an oil change, I basically drove this car for two years without getting the oil changed. The only times I took my car to the mechanic was when I had a flat tire. Now that I am aware of services cars require on regular basis, I believe it was a miracle that my car never totally broke down.

I was a very busy single mother who didn't have the time to go out or date. All my time was spent between home, work, doctor appointments, the grocery store, and going places to pay my bills. My coworkers and I got a long very well, and I did go out with them as a group at least three times within two years.

Although everything seemed to be going on well, it was not easy being in a foreign country all by myself with my son without my extended family. I missed my family deeply, but I was afraid to return to Uganda because I had left my husband and divorced him without the approval of the village elders, given he had paid a dowry. Second, I had secured a job here and could afford to take care of myself and my son, which would have become problematic if I returned home, where it would have been difficult to start all over. Third, I was still afraid of my ex-husband, who refused to accept the separation and even the divorce. During the years after my separation from my ex-husband, he continued to violate the order of protection, often accessing my confidential cell phone number, which I had to change several times. During our divorce hearing, he told the judge whether the court liked it or not, I was still his wife. His failure to accept that it was over between us was scary.

Seventeen

THE INSURANCE GUY

In December 2009 I met a man at Daleo Group Insurance on Main Street, Poughkeepsie, where I often went to clear my monthly auto insurance bill. It was the first time I had seen him there, and he was the agent who processed my payment that day (I had paid my bills two months ahead this day). I had walked in like any regular customer with my two-year-old son.

After this man processed my payment, he asked if my cell phone number was still the same as he handed me my receipt. I responded yes, to which he responded, "I will call to check if it still works." I left, not taking him seriously.

The following evening I received a call from a number I didn't recognize, which I answered. On the other side of the line was a man who introduced himself as the man from Daleo Group Insurance who promised to call to check if my phone worked. I didn't want to be rude so I entertained the conversation. He wanted to know if I was a single mother, to which I said yes. He told me he was a single father of three children. He asked me if I went out to have fun. I told him no, I was too busy to do that. He then went on to give me advice, such as being a single parent didn't mean one couldn't have fun. I thanked him for his advice and called it a night. Andrew continued to call me in the days to come, mostly preaching God's word. He said he could be a pastor, but everything he told me was basically quoting the Bible. It kind of also felt nice talking to him regularly.

A few days later, he asked if he could take me out, and I agreed. Andrew picked me up, and we went to Barnes and Nobles, where he purchased a Bible as a gift for me. The following week he took me to the movies to see *Precious*. After these two dates and regular phone calls in which he often preached, he won my heart. That Christmas I was his guest at their work Christmas party, and I really fell for him deeply. He was a tall and handsome guy in his forties who seemed very mature. I didn't care that he was much older than me; it just felt good to be with someone. I believed with his maturity and Christian-like attitude, he would be caring toward me and my son, and together we would build a great blended family.

Eighteen

Baby on Board Again

Andrew had three children, whom I met a few weeks later. He shared custody with their mother, so he had them every other weekend. They were beautiful and loving children all older than my son with whom we got a long very well. He spent the weekends he didn't have the kids with me and my son either at my apartment or his place. From then on we just never went out again as a couple. He was either at my house, or we were occasionally at his. He got me into a routine of buying him Jamaican food every day with my money and dropping it off to him at work before I left for work.

As we got used to each other, we were planning our future together. He wanted to know if I wanted any more kids, and I told him I just wanted one more since he already had three (two boys and one girl). I hoped to have a girl and be done. Within just three months of us being a couple, he convinced me to have his baby sooner so we could be done with having children. Without thinking twice I agreed and conceived quickly. Before finding out I was pregnant, he would call and tell me to take a pregnancy test.

The day I tested positive, I revealed the result to him over the phone—his response was a laugh and the word "congratulations"! He seemed happy and on board.

As time went by, I began noticing a pattern in which Andrew started conning money out of me. My rent was only $650, and it included cable and hot water; electricity only cost me $60 bimonthly, so I was often okay to help. But his patterns of asking me for money seemed to get worse. Sometimes I sacrificed my own bills to take care of his needs.

It all started by him borrowing $500, which he would promise to pay the following week. He never paid. And then he would borrow $500 again, again with claims that the company he was working for was going out of business, and they were not getting paid. Even though he never paid me back, I just could not deny him.

One day he called me over the phone to beg for rent for his house, which was $1,000. When I told him I didn't have that kind of money, he got angry and yelled that I didn't care about him and his kids and that they were going to be thrown out of the house. Sometimes he would call me to log onto his central Hudson account and pay his electric bill for him, which he would promise to refund me. He never did. At one time he also asked me for money in his mother's name, who he claimed was sick. In addition, when it was time for me to make my monthly car insurance payments, he would ask me to give the money to him and promise to process the payment when he went to work. Months later I learned from the DMV that my insurance had been canceled for lack of payment. I was charged a large sum of money to reinstate it.

Nineteen

FACING DEPORTATION

As I dealt with Andrew, my issues with Gregory resurfaced. My divorce from Gregory took more than a year to become final, and I was granted full custody of our son. Since I had an order of protection against him, my residential address was kept confidential. He was not supposed to contact me by phone; he could e-mail me regarding the child only. However, I was forced to change my number about four times because he kept acquiring it, violating the order of protection. At one time he messaged me on Facebook out of the blue asking if I knew why the mechanics in Syracuse were refusing to fix his car. He believed I had something to do with it. I had no connection with mechanics in Syracuse and neither did I know the auto shops he visited. I was living four hours away from his location and had not been to Syracuse at all since I left. I decided to block him from my Facebook. I couldn't continue to take blame for everything that happened in his life. It was psychologically disturbing for me.

My son and I were pretty much doing well on our own the whole of 2009 through 2010. I had not heard from Gregory for a while except for the few times I had seen him during our divorce hearings. I was represented for free by the Legal Services of Hudson Valley during our divorce proceedings while Gregory represented himself. His attitude in court made the divorce work in my favor because he never wanted to believe that I was about to become his ex-wife. He even told the judge whether they liked it or not, I was still going to be his wife. In the end the divorce was granted, and he was to pay me fifty dollars per month in child support, as I was making more money than him at my current job. Not a single child support payment was ever received to this day, and I let it go. I did not care about child support; I just wanted to be free of him.

I was about six months pregnant with my new boyfriend's child when fellow Ugandan people in the Poughkeepsie area began calling and warning me to watch out because Greg had been calling them demanding my address. They believed with his attitude he was seeking to harm me. A relative of his also called to warn me to be careful, telling me that Gregory was looking for me. He had become homeless, and neither of them here in the United States had agreed to take him in. According to her the university where he was a student had dismissed him. I would later learn in one of his e-mails it was because he failed to pass all the necessary exams required for the PhD program he was pursuing. His visa had been canceled, and he had been given ninety days to leave the country. However, Greg had stayed past the ninety days and refused to leave, demanding that he could not leave without his wife and son.

Shortly after hearing these rumors, I heard from Gregory via e-mails that he forwarded to me. They were e-mail exchanges between him, the university, and a representative from the Ford Foundation offices. He was seeking their help to remove me and my son from the United States. He told them he would not leave the country without us. He claimed my parents were going to ask him for me, yet my family was in fact aware that we had separated. I was so afraid that I e-mailed his university official to explain my part. However, in their response I was also ordered to buy an airplane ticket and leave the country as soon as possible, given my visa depended on his. If I did not leave, I would be facing deportation as well.

As this was going on, Greg had acquired my cell phone number and began calling me and leaving voicemails. In one of the voicemails, he threatened to make it difficult for me and my son if I did not go back to him. During this time, he was already aware that I was pregnant with someone else's child, but he did not seem to want to leave me alone. He was messaging and calling my relatives and everybody he could, telling them that I could not take care of myself and our son and needed them to convince me to go back home to Uganda with him. None of these people cooperated with him. He even got his friend, the Ugandan house flipper in Syracuse, to call my cousin, the nun, on his behalf; instead, this guy told my sister that Gregory had told him that he knew how to shoot guns—basically implying that he could be dangerous.

The following are the e-mail exchanges between my ex-husband, the Ford Foundation representative, his former university, and me:

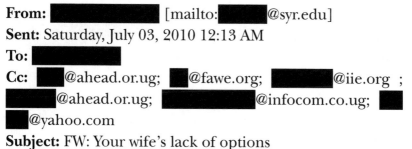

From: ███████ [mailto:███████@syr.edu]
Sent: Saturday, July 03, 2010 12:13 AM
To: ███████
Cc: ██@ahead.or.ug; ██@fawe.org; ███████@iie.org ; ██████@ahead.or.ug; ██████████@infocom.co.ug; ██ ██@yahoo.com
Subject: FW: Your wife's lack of options

Dear ████████ [Ford Foundation representative]

Following my last e-mail about repatriation back home to Uganda, find a better explanation from the immigration department and center for international services at Syracuse. The message forward is below. As I pointed out earlier it is abrupt, and I am required to leave school. Currently my child and my wife are in the United States, and I have legal troubles conducting them. I do not want to be evicted by an immigration agent. Can you please assist me so that I travel back to Uganda with my family. Thank you;

████████████

IFP Program ID: ████████

Sub Account: ████████

From: ██████████████████████@syr.edu]
Sent: Friday, July 02, 2010 3:20 PM
To: ████████████
Cc: ████████████
Subject: re: Your wife's lack of options

Dear ████████ Gregory

The immigration officer did send me back some information. Basically this is what he said:

"As a nonimmigrant, she cannot self-petition to become a Lawful Permanent Resident based on being a battered spouse. Based on the information from our earlier conversation, both the husband and wife appear to be removable. Her status is dependent on his.

Now there may be other circumstances and/or pending petitions that I am not aware of. I would need to conduct internal records checks and interview each of them to make accurate determinations."

So, it is how I first described to you. Fortunate has no legal status since you have no legal status. However, if we reveal her name and your name to the immigration service, it is likely that you will be "detained" (same as being imprisoned) in the Batavia Federal Detention Center (near Buffalo, New York) for an indeterminate amount of time, until you are finally deported. Once deported, you cannot reenter the United States in any status for five years. Fortunate will also be held in a county jail (not in the same prison), and your child will probably be put into foster care. Fortunate will also be deported eventually and will likely be able to take your child with her.

████████, I cannot stress to you enough that *you must go home,* or at least leave the United States. The risks to you are enormous the longer you remain here. I understand that you have asked to serve our new students as a "peer assistant." *Absolutely not.* I cannot give you any "safe harbor" while you remain here in unlawful status.

████████, please accept our offer to buy you a ticket and take you to the airport to leave the country. You can buy tickets for your wife and son if you feel that this is a necessary step to take. But understand that the US justice system will not likely force her to accompany you while the order of protection is still in place.

I suggest (strongly) that you e-mail her the tickets, tell her that you are leaving on such and such a date/time, and that you will inform her father and family in Uganda that you made the arrangements for her and your son to travel back home with you, but that they refused. Then the burden is on her to explain to her father why she did not return to her home.

Also, once you are on the plane to Uganda, I will inform Immigration, and they can go get her (if you want me to do so). However, the idea of her sitting in a jail in Poughkeepsie, and your son in foster care, may not be acceptable to you either. I can at least inform her attorney that I will take this action, and perhaps her attorney can convince her to leave the country. This is definitely in her best interest as well.

I am sorry that this situation has extended and become as difficult as it has become for you. However, it is impossible to correct here in the United States. Please make your plans to leave as soon as possible.

Sincerely,

Dr. ▮▮▮▮▮▮▮▮▮▮▮

Director

From: ▮▮▮▮▮▮▮▮▮▮▮▮▮▮@ahead.or.ug]
Sent: Monday, July 05, 2010 2:25 AM
To: ▮▮▮▮▮▮▮
Cc: ▮▮▮▮▮▮▮▮▮▮▮▮▮▮▮▮▮▮▮▮▮▮
▮▮▮▮▮▮▮▮▮▮▮▮
Subject: RE: Your wife's lack of options

Dear ▮▮▮▮ Gregory

I am sorry about this situation. Could you please write back providing a background to this situation?

Regards

▮▮▮▮▮

From: ▮▮▮▮▮▮▮▮▮▮▮▮▮▮▮@syr.edu]
Sent: Monday, July 05, 2010 4:34 PM
To: ▮▮▮▮▮▮▮
Cc: i▮▮@ahead.or.ug▮▮▮▮▮@iie.org▮▮▮▮@ya-
hoo.com; ▮▮▮▮@ahead.or.ug
Subject: RE: Your wife's lack of options
Dear ▮▮▮▮ [Ford Foundation representative]

Regarding my last e-mail communication, the graduate
school had dismissed me from the graduate program, based
on failure to pass the qualifying exams. I was requested to
leave immediately in March this year. Since it was abrupt, I
had not saved enough to cover transportation including my
family. At the moment I am not enrolled although the dean
of graduate studies has accepted to review my application
for the next spring. Living conditions do not allow me to
stay up to the coming spring if at all my application will be
successful. My status was terminated and as a result I have
to return home and reconsider my decisions from there.

Regarding my family (wife and child), I have not gotten
in conduct with them since they departed in 2008. I have
an order from the court (order of protection against my
child and wife) which has been extended till March 2011. I
have worked hard to reverse this decision but the court and
my wife are not willing to reverse their decision. I cannot
return home without them. I will have another court in July
23 and August 2 for the same case. I need to return with my
family. My wife and child leave in Poughkeepsie, New York,
some 260 miles from my place of study at Syracuse, New
York. She went to Poughkeepsie, to work and ever since she
and her lawyers have refused me to visit them and to see

them. I cannot communicate with them either. My child is now two years and seven months old. Since I have no legal status, that will affect my family as well.

My assistantship was terminated in effective March 2, 2010. I have no other income sources here in the United States. Living away from home for many years, I have not done anything enterprising to raise funds on the side. I have been a sponsored student, and there is no additional fund that I can raise for legal battled in the United States.

The international office had offered to provide me a one-way ticket. However, they are not able to provide for my family and that they are not obliged to suggest to my wife to return. The communication below rose from our discussion of the best available alternative to return.

███████████ Gregory
SUNY-ESF

On Wednesday, July 21, 2010 2:24 AM, ████████████
███@ahead.or.ug> wrote:

Dear ██████ Gregory,

I am sorry about the situation you are in and would encourage you to obtain an air ticket to fly to Uganda. IFP disbursed your repatriation funds in 2006 when Syracuse took up your visa and financial sponsorship to pursue a PhD.

I am sorry to say that we cannot be of any help.

Regards,

██████████

From: Fortunate Vunia [████████@yahoo.com]
Sent: Tuesday, July 06, 2010 4:06 AM
To: ████████████
Subject: ████████████████
Dear Dr. ██████

My name is Fortunate, am writing to you regarding an e-mail that ████████████ (Gregory) forwarded to me between you, him, and ████████████ from Uganda that I will forward to you shortly. I haven't been in contact with ████████ for over two years now and never knew of anything going on in his life, studies, and status in the United States until now when I read the e-mails. I and ████████ separated in 2008 because he was abusing me. Before I left Syracuse, on two occasions he forced me to run out of the house in winter with our infant baby, and the cops were involved and he would end up in the hospital. He had stopped taking his medication for depression and his own relatives living here in the United States helped me move out of our marital home because they feared he would hurt me and the baby since the whole situation had gotten worse and affected my physical appearance. I moved to live with his cousin in Poughkeepsie then but he showed up several times unannounced to harass me until one day neighbors called cops on him. Cops forwarded my issue to Battered Women Services who then helped me through the process of getting order of protection against him.

████████ (Gregory) has never supported me neither our son financially or materially since then even when he was asked to do so. I have worked hard on my own to raise the boy. The only court issue that he is emphasizing here is the divorce, it has been finalized, and he was supposed to fill out a form that the judge required from him for child support.

I am aware that my status here is dependable on his, but I was never aware of what had happened to his status, all I've been working on was the divorce which is due August 2. My job also wished to sponsor me an H1B visa that I was just beginning to process, but if I have to leave, it shouldn't be a problem but *I do not wish to leave here with* ███ as his intention of stressing he cannot live without us is ill. A few months ago, he called my cell phone and left a voicemail threatening me that if I didn't get back to him, he was going to make it difficult for both me and the child, the police have it in their records because I reported, and they heard it. ███ is only insisting he cannot leave here without us because he intends to hurt us in some way.

My family (parents) are aware that I and ███ have been apart for over two years now so he shouldn't lie that my parents want him to return with me. My step mother who's been responsible for me is here in California and can speak on behalf of my family and let you know that my family does not wish me to be with ███ after all I went through. Her name is ███ and her cell-phone number is ███

███ should not insist that he has to leave here with us because we can take care of ourselves including leaving the country. Like you stated if he insists on buying the tickets for us, he can but that's never going to make me accept to go back in the same plane with him. Am sorry for having taken all your time with this e-mail, but I just would like to let my voice be heard. Thanks.

Yours sincerely,

Fortunate

To Fortunate Vunia
CC ████ @esf.edu
07/06/10 at 10:08 PM
Dear Fortunate,

Thank you for your e-mail. I certainly am not in a position to advise you about your marital status or your familial situation. However, as I wrote in my e-mail to ████, which he sent to you, your nonimmigrant status in the United States was terminated when his was terminated, in March 2010. Your order of protection against him does not have any weight against the lack of immigration status.

It is my understanding from ████'s most recent discussion with me that you are likely pregnant at this time (not his child). If that is so, the courts may be lenient with you and not deport you until after the birth of this child. However, the US citizenship status of a child has no bearing upon the legal status of a nonimmigrant parent. As soon as you are medically able to return home, it is likely that you will be deported (once the Border Patrol are aware of your location and status).

Also, although the EAD card, which you have indicating legal employment authorization, was printed by USCIS prior to the termination of ████'s J-1 status, your employment authorization also was terminated when his status as a student was terminated. If you are employed, you are working illegally at this time.

My best advice to you (as it is to ████) is to make plans to leave this country *immediately*, before the Department of Homeland Security finds you and issues you a deportation order. You do not have to leave with ████. If you do leave, you may send me evidence of your departure so that I can confirm this departure with the Immigration Service.

Even if the divorce becomes final in absentia (without you present), you will still have a two-year home residency (home = Uganda) before you could apply to reenter the United States in an H1B status (which you mentioned in your e-mail) or as the spouse of a US citizen or permanent resident (if your plans include remarriage). This two-year home residency requirement was part of ███████'s J-1 visa status, and it is also part of the nonimmigrant visa status of the J-2 dependent.

I tried to contact your lawyer, but it is impossible to get through to her. I left one message, but she never returned the call.

I wish you well in whatever decision you make. However, I must again stress that there is no solution for either you or ██████ in the United States at this time. Your only chance to regain some legal status in your life is to return to Uganda. That is my very strong suggestion, and for your do so in the most immediate future.

Dr. ████████████

Director, Slutzker Center for International Services

Believe it or not, these e-mails would later work in my favor in my struggles, as they served as one of the evidences presented to help me acquire a new visa. I was afraid, confused, stressed out, and feeling helpless. Every immigration attorney I contacted for advice, including the Catholic Charities immigration councilor, had declined to help me, explaining the difficulty of attempting to alter my J-2 status. They all thought it would be impossible due to the two-year rule stamped on my passport that required me to return to my home country for at least two years before I could reenter the United States after my visa expired. I even met with the human resource manager at my workplace to seek any possibilities of applying for a work visa through them. However, my immigration councilor from Catholic Charities decided to reconsider my case after reading the e-mail from Gregory's university that stated that I did not have a future here in the United States and should leave ASAP. She decided to begin the process of filing my case without knowing what the outcome would be. When she submitted my application, still doubting the impact of the two-year rule on my status, she said, "I will just submit it as it is; we will see what happens."

I was still living at my confidential address in Hyde Park with my son when all the above was going on. My apartment was on the second floor of a two-story building, but I lived in the whole building by myself with my son. I did not have any neighbors except for shops that were quite a distance away. One weekend my stepmother and stepsister decided to visit me. I had not seen them since I left Uganda. I picked them up from the train station on a Friday. I had not seen them in years, so we spent that evening and night conversing and catching up. The TV was on, and it was loud in the house as we talked, laughed, and entertained ourselves. We did not hear any noises or knocking from the outside that night.

However, in the morning as we left the house to go out, we noticed dirty, wrinkled papers that had been pushed under the main door. We walked downstairs and noticed that some of the papers had handwritten, signed notes on them—written and signed by my ex-husband. In one of the notes, he stated that he had been there and had gone back to Syracuse, but he promised to be back soon with some millet flour for me. When we opened the door, a plastic bag containing tiny, old toy cars, a birthday card, and a Valentine's

Day card with handwritten notes in them were written to me. It was not my birthday and not Valentine's Day either, but he had written romantic messages to me inside these cards. Hanging on the door was also my old African handbag that I had left in Syracuse years ago. The written notes described in length what a wonderful wife I was, how he had watched me give birth to our son, and how much he loved me. Several years later I would learn that he had put notes on my car as well, which I never saw.

Gregory had located my confidential address and violated the order of protection. The fact that he knew I was heavily pregnant with someone else's child at that very moment, and he was not at all afraid to break the law was so scary. Our divorce had been finalized by this time, but he still called me his wife. He still professed love and wanted to be with me. With all the warning I had received from people he had contacted, I decided to report this violation to the police. A police officer contacted him right away in my presence, but he did not take the officer seriously. He told his cousin that it was my boyfriend who had called him. The assistant district attorney was worried for me and suggested I change my name, which I didn't.

A few weeks later, I heard about his arrest. After serving a few months in jail, he was deported. On the other hand, my visa application went through, and I was granted a new four-year U-nonimmigrant visa. After meeting the three-year requirement of this visa, I was granted permanent residency which meant I could now travel freely.

Twenty

THE INVISIBLE HOUSE

It was time to do our taxes when Andrew decided that I should claim one of his sons along with mine on my taxes, and then we would split my tax return into half, which I did. I got back more than $5,000 in tax returns, and I gave him half of the money. A few weeks later, he returned to me claiming he had found a three-bedroom house for us to move in that was $1,200 per month. He said the owner was his boss, and he required a security deposit of $1,200, which he asked me to pay. He would then pay the first month rent when we moved in. I gave him the money without hesitation. He had even come up with a move-in date. However, when this date approached, he showed up at my apartment with an excuse that the owner needed to fix a few things, and he required another $1,200 to hold the house for us. He asked me to give him that money. When the time to move in came, he would be the one to incur all the expenses for moving. I agreed and basically gave him all my tax refund to secure this house and patiently waited for the second move-in date. Meanwhile, my pregnancy was also progressing.

Andrew lived across the bridge from me. We had planned that we would move in together so we could alternate babysitting the kids. Since he worked a day shift, I was to transfer to work an overnight shift so he could watch the kids at night while I would care for the baby during day and get the kids off the bus on weekdays. Luckily the organization that I worked for was opening a new residential house for their adult services across the river in New Paltz, closer to where we planned to move. I applied for the overnight position there and was offered the job.

When the second move-in date approached, Andrew came up with yet another excuse that the owner of the house had gone on vacation outside of the country, and he didn't know when he would return. Months passed, and there was no good news—just excuses. I even decided that he ask the owner of this house—that I now believe never existed—to refund our money, but it was in vain. I was halfway through my third trimester when I realized I was going nowhere with Andrew. I decided to get a two-bedroom apartment across the river in Highland for $900 per month and move in right away. My working hours were eleven o'clock at night till nine in the morning. I would drop my son off in Poughkeepsie to my Kenyan friend to babysit, drive all the way to New Paltz to work, drive back to Poughkeepsie to pick him up, and then drive home to Highland. Andrew did not spend a single penny on the baby we were expecting, but he gave me his kids' old crib to use. I went to Walmart and shopped for everything my baby would need and waited for my due date.

I didn't tell my coworkers or friends the challenges I was facing; they all thought I was happy in my new relationship. I went into labor at two in the morning while I was at work. I called Andrew to let him know I was in labor and hoped he would come help take me to the hospital, but it wasn't the case. He simply told me to drive myself to the hospital, which I did. Thankfully my son was already at my friend's house for the night, so I stopped home to pick up my bag and drove myself to Vassar Medical Center.

My doctor asked me if I was okay because she could see the amount of painful contractions I was experiencing, but all I had on my face was a smile. She couldn't believe me. When it was morning, Andrew didn't even bother to come to the hospital. He went straight to work and kept calling the hospital to check if I had delivered the baby. I was there all by myself, and God had other plans for me.

While I was in labor at the hospital, my phone rang. It was my Italian friend and coworker. She had never visited me at my home before, but this specific day she called and told me she was close by my home and wanted to stop by to see me. After learning I was at the hospital, she came right away to be by my side and stayed with me the entire time of labor and delivery. The baby was lying high in my womb, so my doctor suggested a C-section. My friend was in the operation theater with me, comforted me, and held the baby to show me as soon as he was delivered. Andrew didn't show up until around midnight. He stayed for a little while and left. He only came very early in the morning or late at night to see us briefly and left.

The day I was discharged from the hospital, I was told I could not drive for at least three weeks because of the medication I was on. This meant I could not drive myself home. I had driven myself into the hospital during labor and had parked my car in the hospital garage. There was no one else I could call to take me home apart from Andrew, who was resistant and told me to call my friends. After insisting there was no friend I could call and that I was needed out by a certain time, he finally agreed to do so. I had him sign the baby's birth certificate papers when he came to take us home. He had named our son Elijah to match my son Ethan and had him take his last name like the rest of his kids. When he came to take us home, he was in a hurry as though he did not want to be spotted in the hospital. He hurried to put the baby in the car and seemed uncomfortable. He even yelled at me at some point. I had him pick my son up from my friend's house, and he finally became relaxed and talked normally once we got home. He had picked up KFC for lunch, which we had together. After that he left and would not return to see us until a few weeks later.

My car was still at the hospital garage after I was released. Andrew had left after dropping us home the day I was released, and he had not returned to check on us. My fridge was empty, and I lacked groceries. My older son was just about three years old, and I could not let him starve. After a few days of calling Andrew for help, he still did not show up, even when I just asked him to pick me and drop me at the hospital garage so I could pick my car on his way to work. Yet he drove by my home every day on his way to and from work. Despite the doctor's order that I could not drive for at least three weeks, I had no choice but to call a cab to take me and my children so I could pick my car up. With fresh wounds, a barely three-year-old child, and a newborn, I drove us to the grocery store and shopped for groceries. I also had to make several trips carrying the groceries upstairs to my apartment.

As if the above experience was not enough, I was to experience further challenges within my home due to Andrew's neglect. A few weeks before I gave birth, I had requested Andrew to follow up with an order I had made for a bed from Big Lots. I had been sleeping on a mattress on the floor ever since I had moved into my new apartment. Since I was heavily pregnant, it was challenging getting up and down from the floor. And after having the baby by C-section, it was even more challenging getting up from the floor to tend to the baby in the crib every night. A few weeks prior to having the baby, I went online and spotted a bed that I liked from Big Lots. It was selling for $280. I told Andrew about it and asked if he could go get it for me if I gave him money. He agreed. Since I really wanted to make sure I got this bed sooner, I gave him $500 and told him to keep the change. He told me to call the store and tell them to bring the bed by the cashier, which I did. That day Andrew never showed up with the bed. The first day passed, and then the second day passed. The third day then turned to a week, and then it was another week—but nothing. He would pick a day and claim a friend of his would be delivering the bed on that day, but nothing happened. Weeks turned into months! That bed was never delivered, and my money was never refunded. He just kept telling me the bed would be delivered on a specific day as months went by, and it never got delivered until I gave up.

Unfortunately, none of my friends knew this was going on. They all thought I was in a happy relationship and settled with a man. Andrew also had a way of controlling me even from a distance. He often told me not to tell people my business. When I went to my friend's house to pick my son, he would call to make sure I didn't spend much time there. He would often tell me to stop spending time in people's homes. Somehow I stayed loyal to his words and never told my friends a single negative thing about him. Sometimes I believed it was my fault because I made myself vulnerable by opening up to him so much about some of the things I had been through in my past relationship. Whenever he took money from me, whether large sums or smaller amounts, he never agreed to take a check. He always insisted on cash even if it meant driving to the bank to get it.

As my eight weeks of maternity leave were coming to an end, I knew there was yet another challenge to come if I had to return to work. Who would watch my children for me? It was clear that Andrew didn't want to be a part of my problems. When I called him about childcare as we had previously planned, he told me to go on craigslist and advertise for a sitter, which I did. When it came to this, I knew I had to do something and seek all the help I could out there, otherwise I would be doomed. I placed an advert on craigslist and also explored the Ulster County social services website online, where I learned I could apply for services online without having to go to their offices.

Right away I applied for childcare for my children and food stamps for them as well. As it turned out, after submitting all the required documents, they both qualified. I was to find my own sitter and pay just $11 weekly while social services took care of the rest. My children would also receive $380 per month in food stamps. As usual I didn't keep this to myself. I told Andrew about the benefits my children would receive, and he started borrowing my children's food stamp card to get groceries for his own home. He only came to my house when he needed money, but he never came just to spend time with us. My son and I often were adopted by unknown families at Christmas who bought us lots of presents through the Battered Women Services. On Christmas Eve 2010, Andrew brought his kids to my house to get their presents from me, and this would be the last time we would see him for months, although he kept in touch over the phone. He would call when he needed to borrow my food stamp card, and I would drop it off for him at his workplace. He also called around the time I filed my taxes asking to share my tax return with him because of the child we had together. It was just my kids and I, and we were doing okay.

Andrew never told his mother about us, yet he claimed his mother dreamed about catching a big fish, which he claimed often happened whenever he was expecting a child. Andrew has said his mother was his only family here in the United States and that he was an only child. She had remarried and lived within the area with her husband. It was so hurtful to me that she didn't even have a clue about her grandchild. I often said to my baby Elijah, who smiled, that over the summer we would try and find his grandma. Every time I told my baby that, he smiled broadly. From the time I began dating Andrew, every time I met a Jamaican, I told them my boyfriend was also Jamaican. But when they asked for his information, none of them seemed to know who he was. Not even the many Jamaicans at my workplace had known him. Andrew spoke perfect English without the Jamaican accent, but he only sounded Jamaican when he was over the phone talking to his family I guess. I started questioning who he really was and wanted to find out, but it seemed difficult. He stopped coming to my place and never entertained the idea of me wanting to come to his place either. When I called him on the phone, he would often not answer; when he did answer, he seemed to be avoiding talking.

Twenty-One

THE REVELATION

My immediate coworker was a Jamaican and didn't know who my boyfriend was even when I gave him all the details he wanted to know. As I waited for spring and summer so I could look for Elijah's grandmother so that he could have a relationship with someone on his father's side, I secretly prayed and wished that one day my coworker would show up and tell me he knew who Andrew was. But as strange as it may sound, really strange and hurtful things began happening.

One day Andrew called to say he wanted to borrow my food stamp card to get his groceries. He told me to drop it off at his workplace, and I agreed, but I did not tell him the time I would be coming. I showed up at his workplace around lunchtime. Normally, when I got there, all I did was call his office line and tell whoever answered the phone to tell him that I was outside. Then he would come out.

I was parking my car by his office when another car driven by a lady pulled in and parked right in front of mine. I made the call. Shortly Andrew came out, but he walked straight to the car parked in front of mine. I was driving a secondhand SUV I had just acquired that Andrew had never seen. The lady in the car parked in front of mine was delivering food for him—the same way I used to do when I was dating him. After receiving his food, as he turned to walk away. He saw me. With a guilty face, he walked to my car window. I felt so lost and didn't know how to react. I felt so betrayed; I had just found out my boyfriend was cheating. I wanted to follow the woman in that car and tell her the truth—that I had just had a baby with this man— but something within me told me not to. I confronted Andrew about it, but he denied and claimed the food was for his boss. I declined to lend him the food stamp card and drove away. I decided to end the relationship, although he continued to call me, always sounding like he still wanted me in his life, yet physically he was never there.

Shortly after finding out Andrew was cheating, another major revelation occurred. One day my coworker, who had no idea who Andrew was, came to work excited. He told me a story about a woman he had met at his other job. His story began with a description of a small town he was coming from known as Clintondale, New York, a town he said he had never been to—he had to use a GPS to get there. He told me he had gone there to visit a new friend who was an LPN nurse and a mother of three kids, but the kids were not there when he visited. As I listened to him, all the descriptions he was giving of this woman sounded like Andrew's ex, the mother of his three kids. As he was still talking, I interrupted him and asked him further and specific questions about her kids and if most likely the kids were with their father. I also asked if she has a specific name, and then told him she sounded like the mother of my boyfriend's kids. Right away my colleague changed the story and didn't say anything further.

A week later, my coworker sat me down and confirmed that I was right about his new friend being the mother of Andrew's children. He had confirmed the truth with her and told her about me and the child I had with Andrew, which she had no clue about. She told my coworker that Andrew at that very moment had another girl in his house who was pregnant with his baby and about to deliver. This meant that at the time I gave birth to Elijah, my boyfriend's other woman was also pregnant. She further revealed that Andrew had ten kids already; mine was the eleventh.

This revelation felt like a miracle to me. Finally uncovering the truth about my baby's daddy was such a huge relief, for I had been in the dark all along. I let Andrew know that I had found out the truth, and he did not deny or admit any of it. Instead he was interested in knowing more about the relationship between my coworker and his ex. From that day forward, his ex would tell my coworker things she knew about him that he would often feed me even if it didn't concern me.

Although I was partly brokenhearted, I decided to move on and care for my children while still hoping and promising my son every day that we would find his grandmother in the spring or over the summer. I never knew her exact address, but Andrew had in the past mentioned the street she lived on, so I planned to go from door to door asking until I found her. Since I was here by myself without my family, I needed the best for my son even though his father seemed not to care about him. I continued to talk to my baby daily, promising him that we would find his grandma, and all he gave me was that angelic smile that I will never forget.

Twenty-Two

Bad News

Three months had passed without Andrew seeing his son. The last time he had seen the baby and spent a little time with him was on Christmas Eve 2010 when he brought his three kids over to my place. We were doing well on our own. My son had just turned six months old, and two of his teeth had started coming in. I was so excited and looking forward to more milestone and brighter days ahead. I had started feeding my baby solid food and was excited about future adventures as he got older.

On the night of March 30, I fed him a cup of applesauce, got him ready, and dropped both my children at the babysitter's at ten thirty in the evening as usual. I left for work. I worked the overnight shift from eleven o'clock till nine o'clock in the morning Sunday night through Wednesday night. This day my baby was healthy and lively. There was no sign of illness or even a slight sign that something could be wrong with him. Around one o'clock in the morning, I received a call from the babysitter stating that my baby was sick and paramedics were on their way. As I was preparing to leave work, the police also called and asked me to meet with them at Vassar Medical Hospital.

All I was thinking at that moment was that my baby had fallen sick and could be admitted in the hospital. I stopped by the sitters to get his diaper bag and quickly went home to pack him a few clothes, diapers, wipes, and formula. When I arrived at the hospital's emergency department, I was taken into a private room that had a table with a protruding white sheet lying over it. This room seemed intentionally designed to break bad news.

As soon as I entered this room, my mind and heart started racing, wondering what to expect. Shortly a doctor walked in and declared that he was sorry, but my baby's heart stopped beating. They asked me if there was anyone I needed to call, but I had no family except for friends, whom I couldn't even think of right away. It felt as if my world just crashed down. I felt a sense of choking in my throat. I broke down and asked to see my son. I didn't want to be the one to call his father, so I gave them his number to do so. The officers picked up my older son and brought him to be with me in the room where Elijah's body lay where we spent that night. My deceased baby's heart was donated to save another. Through the course of the night, I informed a few close friends, who joined me. After the hospital informed Andrew, he called me and stated that he would come in the morning. That morning Andrew called me on his way to work to tell me there was no need for him to come. At that time the hospital was ready to take Elijah's body away, but they were just waiting for his father to arrive. When I told Andrew that the hospital was waiting for him before they could take the body away, he then decided to stop by. He suggested to me that the body be cremated, but I told him I wasn't sure about that. After Andrew arrived and saw the body for a few minutes, it was taken away. I promised to inform him about burial arrangements later.

Lillian, the lady who hosted me when I moved to Poughkeepsie, was one of the friends who stood by me during this difficult time. She opened her home again to me and my son, and so people who wished to come for the funeral could gather. The African community, strangers, and coworkers rallied to morn with me. I provided Andrew with all the information for the wake and the time for the burial according to the program. Several people showed up for the wake, but Andrew was nowhere to be seen. It was around noon, which was the time for the burial, that I received a text message from him stating that he was on his way to the wake but he got sick to his stomach and couldn't handle seeing his son like that, so he turned the car around and went back. I was heartbroken that Elijah's father had denied him from his birth to his death. I cried so much that I wanted to disappear into the face of the Earth.

My response to his father was, "God will deal with you."

A few of us accompanied the funeral van to the burial ground. Pastor Samson Mumbo and elders from the Seventh-day Adventist Church said the prayers, and we left before the body was placed into the ground.

For several weeks following the burial, I cried every night, my tears dropping on the Bible that Andrew bought for me as a present when we started dating. I prayed to God that he could open Andrew's eyes to see that treating a fellow human being the way he treated me and his own child was not right. I prayed that God should not allow him to treat another human being the way he treated us, but rather make him realize his wrongdoing. It was too painful for any human being to be treated this way. After Andrew's failure to attend his son's funeral, I decided to cancel my auto insurance with the company that he worked for and change my number. I also packed his few clothes that were still in my apartment and dropped them off at his door. I didn't want to live at my apartment anymore, so Pastor Samson and his wife took my son Ethan and me in for about a month and a half until I found a new apartment of my own in Poughkeepsie. I also transferred back to my previous work location.

Even though my religious background is Catholic, I continued to attend church at Central Dutchess Seventh-day Adventist Church, where I received a lot of support. Before my son passed, I had dedicated them at this church. In fact, this was the religion that Andrew identified with. I had planned and agreed with him that our son be dedicated. He promised to be there for their dedication. On the Sabbath of the children's dedication, church service could not begin on time because we were waiting for him to arrive. He did not show. After several phone calls and still no show, the children's dedication was postponed to the following week. But as it turned out, it was the same story. Andrew never showed up again, but this time I decided to go forward with the children's dedication in his absence.

One of the church members even stated that "he sounds like a married man." It was such an embarrassment for me, but I kept my head up.

After Elijah's death I drew very close to God. It was the only way I could survive all the pain I was going through. I took a complete spiritual approach to deal with all my troubles. At some point I even decided to get baptized again. However, I would later return to my Catholic faith for personal reasons, although I gained a lot of spiritual guidance from this faith. Listening to worship songs and reciting the miracle prayer daily also kept me going.

The Miracle Prayer

Lord Jesus, I come before you, just as I am, I am sorry for my sins, I repent of my sins, please forgive me. In your Name, I forgive all others for what they have done against me. I renounce Satan, the evil spirits and all their works. I give you my entire self, Lord Jesus, now and forever. I invite you into my life, Jesus. I accept you as my Lord, God and Saviour. Heal me, change me, strengthen me in body, soul, and spirit.

Come Lord Jesus, cover me with your Precious Blood, and fill me with your Holy Spirit. I love you Lord Jesus. I praise you Jesus. I thank you Jesus. I shall follow you every day of my life. Amen.

Mary, My Mother, Queen of Peace, St. Peregrine, the cancer saint, all the Angels and Saints, please help me. Amen.

Twenty-Three

FINAL REVELATION

When people say, "This world is small," it truly is such a small world. I had been using the same mechanic who sold me my very first car from the very beginning since moving to Poughkeepsie. I had often visited his shop with both of my children when I needed work done on my car. During one of those visits, he had a little boy in his shop who was about seven years old. This boy played with my son and baby while we waited for work to be done on my car. The mechanic had introduced him to me as his son. A few weeks after the death of my son, the horn on my car stopped working. I stopped by this mechanic's shop to have it checked. During this visit he asked how my baby was. I told him about his sudden death and that he was half Jamaican like him. He then asked who his father was, and I told him. But his reaction was a laughter. He apologized for laughing and stated that the reason he was laughing was not because I lost my child, but rather because that little boy I found in his shop a while ago who had played with my son was my ex-boyfriend's son—my late baby's father was his real father, and the mechanic was the stepfather. He said the little boy was his stepson but that he treated him like his own. This meant my late son met his half-brother, and my older son played with his little brother's half-brother when we didn't even know it. When I stopped by Andrew's office to cancel my insurance, he complimented me on how good I looked. He also asked me why I had dropped off his clothes by his door.

Instead I said to him, "Oh, by the way, I met your son," and I mentioned his son's name. He just gave me a guilty smile. That was the last time I ever saw him.

Twenty-Four

THE CONFESSION AND APOLOGY

In 2012, exactly a year after losing my child, I began having nightmares in which I could see his father bleeding all over his body and asking me to pour cold water on him. I seemed to have this dream regularly, and I wondered why it was happening. Around the same time, I received a card from donor services for my son's death anniversary. That was when it occurred to me that I should call and check on his father. I hadn't spoken with him in over a year, and there was no way he could contact me either because I had changed my number.

I had learned from his ex through my coworker that she said, "What goes around comes around." Just a month after the death of my son, my late son's grandmother—his father's mother—had been diagnosed with brain cancer. She had only been given about two years to live. His father also seemed to be experiencing other challenges as well, but I was not at all aware of how bad it was.

I was a little disturbed because of the dreams, and so I decided to call Andrew's number but not with my cell phone. I had a house phone that I hardly used, so I decided to call him using that number. His number went through, but there was no answer, and I did not leave any message.

A few minutes later he called back although he didn't know who it was. On finding out I was the one, he was very apologetic. He apologized so much for all the things that he had done to me. He told me all about his mother and everything that he had been through after the death of my child. He said just a month after my baby's death, something happened to his mother. She was either driving or walking and just blacked out, out of the blue. She became terminally ill. He had to take care of his mother. He lost his job and could not afford his cell phone; it was canceled. He couldn't afford his rent and had to move to a smaller, cheaper place. He had just started a new job and turned his number back on when I called him. He claimed he thought I had something to do with everything that was happening to him because of all that he had done to me.

I clearly explained to him that even though I was extremely hurt, I wished him well. I told him that all I did after my son passed on was pray, and I prayed for him too. I told him I had forgiven him a long time ago. He said he also regretted not having told me about the girl he got pregnant while I was having his baby. He said that maybe we could've worked through it. He then went on to advise me to be good to the next man in my life and not treat him badly because of the things he put me through. He also told me where he worked and said I could go and see him. I thanked him for apologizing and wished him well. This conversation brought me closure so I could move on more peacefully.

Several weeks after my conversation with Andrew, I received a call on my house phone. The caller ID showed a company name—Campus Group North America. Coincidentally, one of the companies I had worked for in my past was associated with this name, so I thought it was important that I answered. It turned out to be Andrew again. He wanted to borrow money from me. I couldn't believe him. I boldly told him sorry that I couldn't help him and hung up. I decided to cancel that phone, and we've never been in touch since. This made me question whether he truly ever changed from his old ways, but I was glad never to see him or speak to him again.

Part Three

THE RAINBOW

Twenty-Five

THE POWER OF FAITH

After the death of my son, I decided to work on changing my life around. I also wanted to provide my living son with the best life I could give him after all we had been through together. I got a decent apartment, took up a second job, and went back to school to pursue my master's degree. However, after just one semester, I took a one-year leave of absence to await my eligibility for financial aid. Catholic charities had successfully helped me acquire a U-nonimmigrant visa, but I was still on a three-year probation period before I could qualify for a green card. As a result I couldn't obtain any kind of financial aid to continue my education. I had to wait.

After Elijah's death I found comfort in my faith. I prayed and constantly listened to worship songs that kept me going. One day I sat down and wrote a note to God. In it I expressed gratitude for the blessings in my life. But I asked for one thing: a husband. Then I folded the note up and placed it in my Bible.

Sometime later in early 2012, a friend told me the only way to stop being single was to mingle. I had just gotten off the phone with this friend when I saw a commercial on television of a Christian dating site. I decided to create a profile on an online dating site for Christians. The first name to pop up was a guy named Timothy Higgins. I could click yes, no, or maybe. I paused and remembered some of the online dating horror stories I had seen on television. What should I do? I decided to click yes, and so did Tim. We met in a public place in Hyde Park and quickly learned how much we had in common. Our birthdays were just a day a part. Our jobs were next door to each other. My immediate coworker worked a second job at his job, and he highly approved of him. My other coworker was his high-school classmate. One of our residents was from his childhood neighborhood. When I moved out of my apartment, a close friend and coworker of his had moved in the same apartment.

According to Tim's parents, he came home and told them that he had found the one. He met my son and quickly bonded with him. A few weeks later, he brought both my son and me to meet his parents, who welcomed both of us with open arms. From this day forward, my son and I became a part of their family. Tim's parents became my son's grandpa and grandma, and they were inseparable. My son had not known any extended family his whole life. It had often just been the two of us. Meeting Tim's family was life changing for both of us.

In December 2012 we decided to move in together after Christmas. Tim proposed in August 2013, and we were married on November 2, 2013, in a beautiful, intimate ceremony with around forty guests. On the evening of our wedding, the pastor told us to bring our family Bible to the rehearsal. When I opened the Bible after our rehearsal, the note I had written to God over a year ago asking for a husband fell out. I couldn't believe my eyes! I showed it to family and friends who were present. It was a wow moment.

After our wedding ceremony, a rainbow appeared while our wedding pictures were getting taken by the Hudson River. It was captured in our pictures. On August 19, 2014, we welcomed our first child, a girl we named Serenity. In August 2015 we purchased our first three-bedroom home, and God continued to bless us.

A rainbow appeared in the sky after our wedding ceremony.

"Cheers to the future," at our wedding reception.

With part of the family on our wedding day.

In this picture is my friend Maria, my former English-conversation group leader from Syracuse, New York, about whom I wrote in the earlier chapters. She somehow found out about my son's death and surprised me by attending his funeral. When she came to greet me after the wake, I had to ask her at least three times to confirm if it was her. My son's death reunited us, and she would years later attend my wedding.

In summer 2015 I visited my family in Uganda for ten days. It had almost been nine years since I had last seen them. The morning of my flight, I received a phone call from my step-sister telling me my eldest brother, Luke, had passed away from an unknown sudden illness. I was of course devastated because I had just spoken to him for the first, and last time in almost nine years, a week prior. I had called my mom when he happened to be present, and she handed him the phone so I could say hello to him. At that time, he was not ill. He thanked me for some clothes I had sent him in the past, and I had asked him if he needed me to bring him anything from the United States. He had asked for a cell phone which I happily bought for him, and already packed in my travel bag. Due to this tragic event, my plans for my visit changed. Upon my arrival my brother had already been buried. I spent the rest of my visit at home with my family.

After my departure there was a gathering between my ex-husband's family and my family to settle the issues that had transpired during our marriage. I was not there to defend myself, but I was told he said I left him because I was making more money than him. Some of his family members also believed that I took everything from him and left him with nothing. Yet when I left, I had quit my job, and I did not carry any belongings. He also blamed his cousin who hosted me for our failed marriage. His family demanded that the dowry they had paid be returned. According to witnesses at some point, the argument between the two families was so heated that a fight almost broke out.

The issues weren't settled; it was postponed until I could be there to give my side of the story.

Twenty-Six

THE REPORTER FROM THE *POUGHKEEPSIE JOURNAL*

In fall 2015 I was learning about loss and grief in my helping skills class in graduate school. I had been thinking about my late son so much and feeling guilty that I had not been able to visit his grave. I was also feeling very guilty and disturbed that I had donated his heart to save another life, yet I had not kept his memory alive. I thought about what I needed to do to find his grave and have a headstone placed on it. Incredibly, God had other plans. Within the same time frame, I received an e-mail from a *Poughkeepsie Journal* reporter, who asked me to give him a call. He had been searching for me. What followed his e-mail is detailed in the newspaper article below.

Part of my story on the front page of the *Poughkeepsie Journal.*

The story of a
mother, a cop and
a baby's lost grave

EVERY YEAR, HUNDREDS
OF PEOPLE LIKE ELIJAH
WILLIAMS ARE LAID TO REST
IN LOCAL CEMETERIES, THEIR
FAMILIES UNABLE TO PAY
FOR BURIAL SERVICES.

John Ferro, Poughkeepsie Journal

'I thought I had lost him forever'

Fortunate's Unfortunate Fortunes

Editor's note: This is the story of a grieving mother looking for her son's grave, the police officer who tried to save the boy's life and how they were brought back together at the child's final resting place by Poughkeepsie Journal reporter John Ferro.

Fortunate Higgins drove into LaGrange Rural Cemetery, still unaware of where her infant son had been buried.

The 34-year-old Hyde Park resident had tried to find her son's grave before with no luck.

Elijah Williams died in 2011 of sudden infant death syndrome, or SIDS. The 6-month-old had been laid to rest through an indigent burial program.

(Photo: Patrick Oehler/Poughkeepsie Journal)

But, county programs do not cover the cost of a headstone. And when his mother had returned months after the funeral, she had been unable to find any marker in the cemetery's 10 grassy acres.

"I thought," she would say later, "I had lost him forever."

Now she was back. Unknown to her, Town of Lloyd police Lt. James Janso, who had tried to save her son that night more than four years ago, had been visiting the baby's grave for years.

In an unlikely turn of fate, they were about to meet again.

Fortunate opened the car door and fell to her knees. Janso put his arm around her.

"Thank you so much. Thank you so much," she said, sobbing.

"I checked on him every year," Janso said.

"This," Fortunate said holding a small box filled with mementos, "is all I have of him."

Then the mother and the lieutenant rose to their feet. Janso led her a short distance to her son's grave.

"Is this the one?" Fortunate said. "Oh my goodness. I didn't even know."

She fell to her knees again and cupped the little, metal marker.

"Oh my God," she said, "he's right here."

'Not one I will forget'

The call for an unresponsive infant went out at 1:04 a.m. on March 31, 2011. Lloyd's police department, like others, has a policy directing its officers to respond to all medical calls.

Janso was among the officers and paramedics who arrived at the home on New Paltz Road.

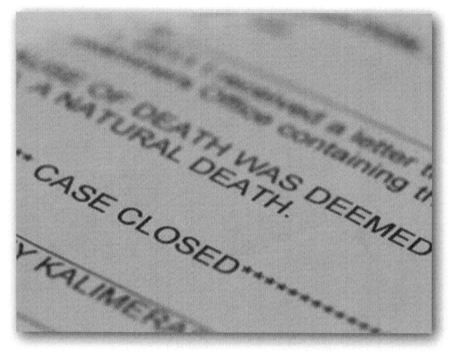

(Photo: Patrick Oehler/Poughkeepsie Journal)

Inside, a babysitter was kneeling on the floor, performing CPR. The officers and paramedics took over, swapping out.

Two breaths. Then, 30 chest compressions, using two fingers. Over and over.

The boy was taken to Vassar Brothers Medical Center.

Janso has done CPR many times on adults. Some have made it. Some have not. It's part of the job.

This was different.

"Not one I will forget," he said.

A few weeks later, Lloyd police would file a one-page supplement to its investigation report. A final autopsy and toxicology analysis overseen by the Dutchess County Medical Examiner's Office had determined the cause of death to be SIDS. It is the medical term used to unexplained deaths of seemingly healthy infants during sleep.

"A natural death," the report reads. "Case closed."

A dowry of cows, then threats

Fortunate had come to America from Arua, a town in northwest Uganda. Idi Amin, the country's infamous former dictator, spent his childhood years there.

(Photo: Courtesy photo)

Shortly after finishing college in Uganda, she was introduced to a man by a relative. Both were from the same tribe. The man had been studying in the United States, and returned to Uganda to marry Fortunate and bring her to America with him.

The traditional ceremony was overseen by elders from each of their villages. The groom paid a dowry of cows to Fortunate's family.

Fortunate obtained a student visa and in January 2007, the newlyweds flew to New York, where they settled in Syracuse. A son, Ethan, was born not long after.

But it soon became clear to Fortunate that her husband suffered from mental illness. Paranoia. He made threats.

She feared for her life, and in 2008, she fled to Poughkeepsie to stay with a friend. A divorce followed.

Sometime after, Fortunate met another man. They dated for a short time before separating. Elijah Williams was born on Sept. 28, 2010.

A small box of memories

Fortunate was working an overnight shift in New Paltz, at one of the Anderson Center for Autism's adult residences, when she got a call from her babysitter.

Elijah was sick, the babysitter said. Paramedics were on the way. A short while later, police called. They told her to come to Vassar Brothers Medical Center. They didn't say why.

Fortunate stopped at home in Highland to fill a diaper bag with items. When she arrived at the hospital, the doctors took her into a private room.

Fortunate stayed with her son's body until he was taken away later that morning.

Sometime in the early morning hours, a hospital staff member brought a white box. The hospital has a support program for bereaved parents and their families after the death of a baby. One aspect of that program is the gift of a memory box.

(Photo: Patrick Oehler/Poughkeepsie Journal)

Inside, were items. A mold of Elijah's hand. His hand and foot-prints on a paper card. A small plastic bag containing a lock of his hair. A blank journal with the title, "I Will Remember."

Members of the local Ugandan and Kenyan communities, as well as friends and strangers, rallied around Fortunate. There was a wake, and then the burial. The Rev. Samson Mumbo of Central Dutchess Seventh-Day Adventist Church spoke.

When prayers were done, they left. Elijah's coffin had not been placed in the ground.

Fortunate did not return for some time. Indeed, the concept of traveling to visit a family member's grave was foreign.

"In my culture, cemeteries are not places people visit often and people are mostly buried within the home environment," she said.

When she came back, she looked for a headstone. There was none.

She padded the grassy earth with her feet, searching for a soft spot or any sign of a recently dug grave.

She called the funeral home. They had no information about a headstone, since one had never been placed.

She had taken a picture during the burial that she thought might help her locate the grave, but her computer had crashed and she lost it.

"I didn't know what to do," she said, "so I left it the way it was. Since then, the memory box (from Vassar Brothers) was what I held close every time I needed to connect with my son."

Indigent burials

Every year, hundreds of people are laid to rest in local cemeteries, their families too poor—or in some cases unwilling—to pay for burial services. For them, there is Section 141 of the state social services law.

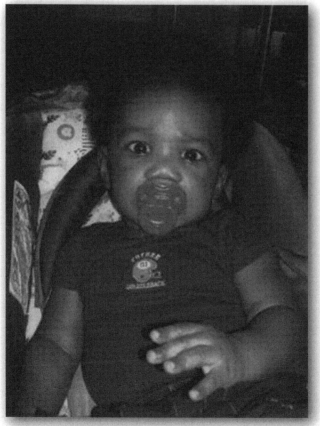

(Photo: Courtesy photo)

The law mandates that local public welfare districts be responsible for covering the cost of burials whenever "the deceased leave no funds or insurance sufficient to pay the expense of (the) burial and there are no known relatives, friends or personal representatives liable or willing to become responsible for such expense."

Municipal support for indigent burials dates at least as far back as fourth-century Rome, according to the National Funeral Directors Association. Under Constantine the Great, the first Christian emperor, even the poorest of the poor were followed to the grave by a cross-bearer, monks and acolytes.

On average, the Dutchess County and Ulster County programs account for a total of about 280 burials each year.

Elijah Williams was one of them.

A small, metallic marker

Some months after the funeral, Janso came across Elijah's obituary. It said the boy had been buried in LaGrange. The lieutenant knew the area, having lived nearby for a period of time.

Janso, 47, has two children, a teen and toddler. He joined the Lloyd department in 1990. He grew up in Highland, the descendant of Czechoslovakian and Irish immigrants. His Czech grandfather had worked as a coal miner in Pennsylvania.

After reading Elijah's obituary, Janso wanted to visit the grave. What a grief-stricken, single mother still relatively new to the country had been unable to do, the seasoned, local police officer managed with a couple of phone calls.

(Photo: Patrick Oehler/Poughkeepsie Journal)

Soon, he was standing before a small, metallic marker.

"That saddened me," he said, "to see that."

Janso kept coming back, typically around the holidays. Sometimes snow had flattened the marker. Other times, grass clippings had piled up around it.

"Eventually, you couldn't even find his grave," he said.

Each time, the police officer fixed things up. He didn't know if Elijah's family was still in the area, or if it was simply too painful for them to go. Grief has no playbook, no standard operating procedure.

A few weeks ago, Janso was talking to me about an unrelated case. Within the context of that conversation, Janso mentioned Elijah's story.

Janso said he was thinking of passing the hat around the department to raise money for a headstone.

"Nothing elaborate," he said. "Just a reminder that he is there. Not just a typed name, on a piece of paper, in a little sleeve."

I asked if I could write about it.

Janso said yes.

I asked Janso if he would reach out to the surviving family members.

Janso said he would, but later he hesitated.

What would he say? How would he explain it?

In the meantime, I began to search for Elijah's mother.

A letter to God

After Elijah's death, Fortunate found comfort in her faith.

She prayed. She listened to worship songs.

"That kept me going," she said.

One day she sat down and wrote a letter to God.

In it, she expressed gratitude for the blessings in her life. But she asked for one thing: A husband. Then she folded up the letter and placed it in her Bible.

Sometime later, in early 2012, a friend told her the only way to stop being single is to mingle. So Fortunate created a profile on an online dating site for Christians.

The first name to pop up was somebody named Timothy Higgins. She could click yes, no or maybe.

She paused. She remembered some of the online dating horror stories she had seen on television.

What to do? She clicked yes. So did he.

They met in a public place in Hyde Park and quickly learned how much they had in common. Their birthdays are just one day apart. Their jobs are next door to each other. Fortunate's former residence had been in Tim Higgins' childhood neighborhood.

When she had moved out of her apartment a close friend and co-worker of his had moved in.

Was it providence?

On the night before their wedding, during the rehearsal, Fortunate opened her Bible. Out came the letter.

On Aug. 19, 2014, they had their first child, a girl.

An email from a reporter

On Dec. 4, Fortunate received an email from me. It was about her son, a police officer and a headstone.

(Photo: Patrick Oehler/Poughkeepsie Journal)

She called back immediately.

Without being asked, Fortunate poured out the details. The death. A burial. The grief. A search.

I interrupted her.

"I have some information for you," I said.

I told her a police officer had been visiting her son's grave for years, and that I was meeting the officer later that day.

"Oh my goodness!" she said.

Then I called Janso back. I told the lieutenant I had found the mother, and that she had been searching for her son's grave.

"Are you (kidding) me?" Janso yelled into the phone, using a different word.

Now, in just a few hours, Janso would show her the grave. The last time he had shown her anything, it had been an autopsy report.

Serenity

The sun was beginning to set when Elijah's mother arrived in the cemetery with her husband and their daughter.

Through the windshield of their car, you could see something in her lap. The memory box.

The lieutenant and the mother embraced. "Don't make me cry," he told her.

They walked to the grave.

The lieutenant pulled out a tiny Christmas wreath, maybe two inches across, and propped it up against the small marker.

(Photo: Patrick Oehler/Poughkeepsie Journal)

Fortunate said that when she told her friends where she was going, there was another revelation. Some of them had been raising money secretly to purchase a headstone. Two-hundred dollars, so far, she said.

Later, she would give it to Janso. A headstone will be placed sometime in the New Year.

The Higgins' daughter bounced playfully around her half-brother's grave, too young to understand it all.

"What's her name?" I asked her parents.

"Serenity."
John Ferro: 845-437-4816; jferro@poughkeepsiejournal.com; Twitter: @PoJoEnviro

Online
To view a video of the reunion of Fortunate Higgins and Lt. James Janso at Elijah Williams' grave, go to www.poughkeepsiejournal. com.

Part two of my late son's story on the front page of *Poughkeepsie Journal.*

Lloyd police officer leads fundraising effort for site of Highland baby's indigent burial

(Photo: Patrick Oehler/Poughkeepsie Journal)

Where once only a small, metal marker denoted Elijah Williams' final resting place, now there is a gleaming new headstone.

The memorial was placed earlier this month by Town of Lloyd police Lt. James Janso, one of the first-responders who tried saving Elijah five years ago.

The 6-month-old Highland boy died on March 31, 2011 of sudden infant death syndrome.

"I think," Elijah's mother, Fortunate Higgins said, "God placed (Janso) on Elijah's path and on our path for a reason."

The headstone is the most recent development in an improbable story marked by two chance encounters—one tragic, the other restorative. The story was detailed in a Poughkeepsie Journal report, "The mother, the cop and a baby's lost grave," on Christmas Day.

(Photo: Patrick Oehler/Poughkeepsie Journal)

Janso, moved by Williams' death and word that the boy's simple burial had been through Ulster County's indigent burial program, had begun raising money for a headstone.

Higgins, unaware of Janso's efforts, had lost track of where her son's grave was at LaGrange Rural Cemetery, his little marker sometimes displaced by snow or wind, or obscured by grass clippings.

The last time Janso had seen Higgins, a 34-year-old Ugandan native now living in Hyde Park, it had been to present the mother with the autopsy results.

(Photo: Patrick Oehler/Poughkeepsie Journal)

They came together again in December, after a Poughkeepsie Journal reporter contacted Higgins and informed her of Janso's plans.

The account of their emotional meeting resonated with readers.

Offers of donations, from both local and out-of-state residents, came into Janso's and the Poughkeepsie Journal's offices.

Janso said he had to turn away most of the donations. Nearly all of the money, about $1,200, was quickly raised between Janso's family, other Lloyd police and Higgins' friends—enough to pay for the headstone, as well as flowers for two years from Always in Bloom Flower Shop in LaGrangeville.

The headstone was fashioned by Weidner Memorials of Highland. LaGrange Rural Cemetery waived labor costs for the foundation.

Janso said he chose the design at the base of the stone, which depicts a scene reminiscent of a Beatrix Potter tale. Potter is best known for her Peter Rabbit and other stories.

"Just the innocence of childhood," he said.

He said he asked Higgins if she wanted to change the design.

"She could do whatever she wanted and I would take care of it," he said.

Higgins made no changes.

"It's comforting for me," the mother said, "to know that he has a beautiful resting place, and I can always come here any time to visit."

Higgins said she wants to bring one other person to the grave. Her first son, Ethan, was born three years before Elijah.

(Photo: Courtesy photo)

Ethan, now 8, struggled in local schools. He has spent the last year living with family and going to school in Uganda.

"He never really understood that Elijah was gone and never coming back, until he was about 5 or 6 years old," his mother said.

Sometimes, Ethan would ask questions about what happened. "I wish Elijah was here," he would say.

Mostly, he suffered in silence.

"Now that there is a headstone," she said, "I'm really excited for him, because I know that is how he is going to get his closure. I can't wait to take him there when he comes back."

John Ferro: 845-437-4816, jferro@poughkeepsiejournal.com, Twitter: @PoJoEnviro

Twenty-Seven

Double Blessing

Between 2013 and 2014, I fulfilled my dream of constructing a decent three-bedroom, two-bathroom house for my family in the village in Uganda. I wanted to fulfill my father's dream that had failed after the accident that left him brain damaged and our family's life ruined. I can proudly say it was a success! Although we still lack clean water and electricity in our village, life for my family in Uganda has improved for the better. Below is a before-and-after view of an area at my parents' home in the village.

Before the construction.

After (construction in progress).

After Serenity's birth I returned to school in spring 2015 to complete my master's degree. My husband and in-laws watched the kids while I attended classes. I worked full time at night and attended classes twice—sometimes thrice—a week, in the evenings and on weekends. I graduated successfully in December 2016 with a master's degree in professional studies in humanistic and multicultural education. During my final semester, we found out we were expecting our second and last child, a boy, whom we named Timothy Jr. The graduation ceremony took place on May 19, 2017, while I was nine months pregnant. I received the Outstanding Graduate Award and graduated with honors. I was *blessed* with a master's degree and a baby!

My master's degree commencement, 05/19/2017.

Me, my husband, and daughter Serenity on my graduation day.

After separating from my ex-spouse, Gregory, back in 2008, it was clear my only opportunity to gain my independence from his J visa status was to enroll in school and change my visa status. However, back then he wanted to make this impossible for me, so he held my academic documents and took them back to Uganda when he visited after our separation. I fought back by having one of my influential family members pressure him to surrender them, which was a success. They were mailed back to me from Uganda. If I had allowed him to control my destiny by holding my academic documents, I wouldn't have graduated today.

In fact, when I enrolled in graduate school, I was extremely scared that I wasn't going to make it because my undergrad was in the British education system. Most of the immigrants I knew of African background abandoned their previous education to start all over again when they moved to the United States. I chose to evaluate my transcripts and convert them into the American education system. The evaluated outcome did not quite meet the required GPA for the program I applied for, but thankfully the dean of graduate studies understood the British education system very well, and she thought my evaluated results were unfair. She took her time to compare the two and decided that she would admit me to graduate school based on my original transcript, on the condition that I performed well in my first semester. She also encouraged me that she knew I could do it. Her words stayed with me throughout the years that I worked extra hard.

I was also greatly inspired by my academic advisor, Dr. Terry Murray, and professors Dr. Nancy Schniedewind and Priscilla Prutzman, who often made me feel valued in the classroom. My classmates also valued me despite my different cultural background. Their acceptance helped me fit in and do my best.

As I walked the stage on the day of commencement, the dean of graduate studies hugged me and told me how proud she was of me. I am forever grateful to each and every one who contributed to my academic success. Life goes on.

In Loving Memory
ELIJAH T. WILLIAMS
September 28, 2010
March 31, 2011

I am the WAY, the TRUTH, and the LIFE. John 14:6

The Lord is my shepherd; I shall not want. He maketh me to lie down in green pastures; he leadeth me beside still waters. He restoreth my soul; he leadeth me in the paths of righteousness for His name's sake. Yea, though I walk the valley of the shadow of death, I will fear no evil; for thou art with me. Thy rod and thy staff they comfort me. Thou preparest a table before me in the presence of mine enemies; thou annointest my head with oil; my cup runneth over. Surely goodness and mercy shall follow me all the days of my life; and I will dwell in the house of the Lord forever.

William G. Miller & Son Funeral Home, Inc.

About the Author

Fortunate Higgins lives with her husband and family in Hyde Park, New York. She received her bachelor's degree in industrial and fine arts at the Margaret Trowel School of Industrial and Fine Arts of Makerere University in Uganda. Higgins received her master's in professional studies in humanistic and multicultural education from the State University of New York at New Paltz. Upon graduation, she received the Outstanding Graduate Award from the university.

References

Ferro John, "The story of a mother, a cop and a baby's lost grave," *Poughkeepsie Journal*, December 25, 2015, www.poughkeepsiejournal.com/story/news/local/2015/12/24/lloyd-police-grave-mother-elijah/76685698/

Ferro John, "A baby's lost grave gets a headstone," *Poughkeepsie Journal*, April 28, 2016, www.poughkeepsiejournal.com/story/news/local/2016/04/28/elijah-williams-grave-headstone/83509094/

Wallace, Susan Helen. *Saint Bakhita of Sudan: Forever Free*. Boston: Pauline Books, 1940.

Made in the USA
San Bernardino, CA
26 June 2020